WILL RUN FOR
DOUGHNUTS

The Montclair Bread Company Cookbook

RACHEL WYMAN

Photography by Brad Barket

Andrews McMeel
PUBLISHING®

TO KYRA

For encouraging me to fry the first doughnut, run the first mile, and write the first chapter.

Contents

Chapter 3
DOUGHNUTS 67

The MBCo Classics

Alternate Endings

Quick Doughnuts

Glazes and Fillings

Chapter 4

COMMUNITY FAVORITES 119

Chapter 5

RECIPES FROM QUARANTINE 145

FUELED BY DOUGHNUTS AND MORE

Nine months after I opened Montclair Bread Company in Montclair, New Jersey, a prominent town just outside New York City, business was stale. I opened the bakery in 2012 to support my struggling family but found that the stress and long hours actually wreaked havoc on my bank account and my already failing marriage.

I had spent years rising before dawn to perfect the combination of flour, water, yeast, and salt for some of the country's most well-known bakeries. Now I had the bread to prove it, and I was excited to sell it to my neighbors. But on a good weekend day, only thirty people trickled through my door.

The owner of the corporate recipe development company I worked for during the week had gifted me a beautiful copper pot. I lugged it to the empty bakery one cold Sunday morning in January 2013. My baker and friend, Kyra Wilder, took one look and said, "You know, this will hold heat really well. It would be perfect for frying something. Have you ever made doughnuts?"

I thought, "Why not?" I had nothing else to do. I eyed our brioche dough, remembering that French cooks fry brioche to make beignets. After some improvisation with a shallow pot and an induction burner, I had made three dozen fluffy rings. I dredged them in cinnamon and sugar. Kyra and I, along with two other retail employees, ate half of them while they were still warm from the fryer.

I put the rest out for sale. This was a risky move because my customers often begged for healthy foods, the specialty of the previous bakery that had occupied this location. I was certain they would tar and feather me for my flagrant display of white flour, sugar, and butter. At best, the doughnuts would just go stale by the end of the day.

To my surprise, the doughnuts sold out in three minutes flat. Kyra and I looked at each other. "I guess we should make these again next week?" I said.

The bakery didn't have room for a stovetop, so I heated the oil in the copper pot on top of a small electric burner. I could fit only five doughnuts at a time into the pot. I had to wait a full minute in between batches for the oil to recover enough heat to fry the next five. The dough would often overproof before I could get it into the oil. But somehow, whatever I put on the counter was purchased before I could turn around.

Over the next few months, thirty customers turned into 130, and they all wanted doughnuts. I began to dub the late afternoon/early evening shift the "apology shift," because all those employees did was apologize that we had sold out of doughnuts.

On Valentine's Day that year, I made the first Boston cream doughnut, heart-shaped and filled with homemade custard. For St. Patrick's Day, I made an Irish Car Bomb doughnut, covered in a Guinness glaze and topped with a Baileys Irish Cream–stuffed doughnut hole.

By Mother's Day, the line stretched to the end of the block. By then, I had also upgraded from my copper pot to a tabletop home fryer. Now I could fry six doughnuts at a time, and I didn't have to wait for the oil to reheat between batches. I still couldn't keep up, though. I knew we would sell out before the last person in line reached the door.

I locked myself in the bathroom and called my grandmother, Mom-Mom, or "Mombo," as my young daughter called her. Mombo was also a baker. She had started this whole thing by handing me a piping bag filled with buttercream when I was three.

"What do I do? They're going to be disappointed and angry," I sobbed.

"You pull up your big girl panties, and you make more next week," Mombo replied.

So I did.

I scraped together enough money to order an even bigger doughnut fryer, the type that was usually used for frying funnel cakes at a carnival. It could fit twelve doughnuts at a time, but I had to wait for it to ship from Europe, and it wouldn't arrive in time for Father's Day.

I didn't want to disappoint a line of eager customers again, so I purchased a second French home fryer. However, my bakery's electrical system was so outdated I couldn't plug both fryers in next to each other. They had to be used on opposite ends of the bakery; otherwise, they would blow a fuse, and then someone would have to navigate the treacherous steps down to the spider-filled basement to flip the breaker.

Again, we sold out. We apologized. We got up again the next morning and made even more. And more.

And over the next few years, my sleepy little spot turned viral. Customers lined up again and again. My doughnuts appeared in the *New York Times*. The Food Network's *Donut Showdown* asked me to be a contestant, and my tres leches doughnuts and I won! I watched our doughnuts scroll by on countless social media feeds, including those of Martha Stewart and Lin-Manuel Miranda. Actress Mindy Kaling begged her New York–based agent to ship doughnuts to her in L.A., and her photo of the box appeared in *People*.

As my business grew, customers and the media assumed I was a confident, competent businesswoman at the head of a thriving bakery. No one could have imagined the obstacles I had to overcome to get to where I was.

I learned to bake as a child when I wasn't navigating absentee parents and financial insecurity. I took notes in culinary school as I battled anxiety and depression. Once I began baking professionally, I fought my way up the ranks in a male-dominated and often shockingly sexist industry. After I married, I struggled to support my husband and three young children.

As my star rose and rose, so did the emotional and verbal abuse from my husband, which continued until I gathered the courage to file for divorce.

It was in Montclair Bread Company that I found my community. I began to notice that my most enthusiastic doughnut fans were runners, who would finish their long runs at the bakery and then carbo-load. To commemorate our Facebook page getting 4,000 likes in 2013, we threw together a 4K run. To my surprise, I ran and enjoyed it. Running began to bring me energy, friends, and community.

Eight months later, I launched the Fueled by Doughnuts Running Club, my way of giving back to my community. We now end our runs at Montclair Bread's new headquarters: an old DMV inspection station that I turned into a 1,300-square-foot retail bakery and production space, along with an 800-square-foot patio with outdoor seating. Our annual races sell out within minutes of registration opening.

We also sell out cooking classes, baking classes, and camps. I began baking pizzas on the weekends out of my wood-fired oven, alongside live music. And my three children and I began to rebuild our family life, with the help of a new partner, Brad Barket.

Then in August 2018, I was 38 miles into a 40-mile bike ride when someone opened his car door right in front of me.
I swerved around it, but I lost control of my bike. My wheels slipped out from under me, and my hip slammed against the pavement.

My pelvis was shattered. I was bleeding internally and nearly died from my injuries. After an emergency surgery of more than eight hours, a team of doctors reconstructed my bones with the help of a dozen screws and a couple metal plates.

Doctors predicted I wouldn't run for at least a year. I couldn't wait that long. I continued to put one foot in front of the other, making the most of each step, each day, as I got stronger. I never went outside of the doctor's restrictions, but I worked as hard as I could within them. I took my first unassisted step eight weeks after the accident.

By December, I was running my own 5K Doughnut Run alongside the governor of New Jersey, Phil Murphy. And when the federal government shut down the next month, I was in a position to help: my children and I made and packaged hundreds of doughnuts and drove them to Newark airport for the unpaid TSA workers.

Then in 2020 came the coronavirus pandemic. My town went into quarantine. I went into survival mode, laying off staff and selling grocery staples such as fresh produce, flour, and eggs out of my bakery. I began sharing my recipes online, which brought me a lot of comfort. This turned into town-wide virtual bake-alongs that my regular customers said brought them great comfort, too. Those led me to write this book.

I want to share my favorite recipes with you, but I also want to tell you my story, the story behind these recipes, like Mombo's Carrot Cake and Montclair Bread Company's infamous Classic Brioche Doughnuts. The path to success isn't a straight line, and it has a few uphill climbs. In fact, sometimes when you think your body can't handle one more peak, you make it over the top. Resilience is getting up every morning, putting one foot in front of the other, and remaining in constant forward motion.

Baking Basics

There are two things I've never had much of: money and space.

My grandmother's kitchen, where I learned to bake, was smaller than many bathrooms. Its L-shaped counter included a small sink, a dishwasher, and a workspace with a cabinet underneath that housed nesting bowls and casserole dishes. My grandmother kept a bar stool in the bend of the L where she could sit and have everything she needed at an arm's reach. Her tools—pots, pans, mixer, griddle, coffee mugs, everything—had a very specific home. She counted the silverware in the tiny drawer by the sink each night to make sure not a single fork was missing. There was no excess, no gimmicks, only what was essential. Her paring knife was used so often the blade was worn down into an arch.

From my grandmother's kitchen to a basement apartment in Queens and finally to a 600-square-foot bakery on Walnut Street, I struggled as money and space continued to limit my ability to stockpile kitchen tools. However, I think this was a good thing. The fewer tools you have, the more organized you can be in the kitchen. Everything gets used. Everything has more than one purpose. You will not find a garlic press or citrus juicer in any of my drawers!

One thing about working in a bakery: you learn to cook without a stove. You learn to be resourceful and use the tools you have. I have rarely eaten as well as I did when I worked the overnight shift at Amy's Bread from 2004 to 2008. I'm not just talking about the treats we were baking for customers, though. When we finished the night bake, while most of the world was still asleep, we took turns helping prepare Sarath's Sri Lankan curry, Lao's Chinese dumplings, Miguel's tamales, Nick's chicken wings, and José's oxtail stew. We did all of this using the bread oven, the convection oven, and the steam wand from the espresso machine. A note to my friend Amy Scherber: I'm so sorry we abused that pricey machine to heat our soups and sauces!

Today at Montclair Bread Company, we have two induction burners but no stovetop. I can make just about anything inside an oven, from grilled cheese sandwiches to white rice. Rather than using six pots, I use one or two pans because that's all the oven space I have. Having less space, fewer tools, and less equipment has made me more resourceful, more inventive, and more organized.

Tools I Can't Live Without

Below, you will find the items I consider essential to have in a baker's kitchen, or any kitchen, really. These are in no particular order.

Chef's Knife: I have a standard 8-inch blade that I've had since culinary school. I use it for EVERYTHING, except for when I use my serrated knife . . .

Serrated Knife: I use this for slicing baked breads and tomatoes. It's also known as a "cake knife," which is really a long, straight "bread knife." Sometimes the knives marketed as a "bread knife" are too short to make it through a big, hearty loaf. Look for something that's at least 8 inches long.

Bench Knife: This is a rectangular metal blade, about 4 inches wide, with a wooden or plastic handle. It is used to cut raw dough and is great for scraping gunk off tables, too.

Bench Scraper: This is just like the bench knife but made of plastic. It bends to curve around the inside of a mixing bowl to scrape down the sides or remove every last bit of yum. I have also discovered that a plastic bench scraper is the absolute best tool for removing ice from my windshield in the winter. I keep at least one in my glove compartment.

Offset Metal Spatula, 8 to 13 inches: It has a long, narrow metal blade that's great for icing cakes.

Pastry Brush: This can be used for dusting flour off the surface of dough, brushing egg wash onto brioche, or spreading oil on focaccia. A standard 1½-inch wooden brush with boar hair or nylon bristles is optimal.

Rolling Pin (or a wine bottle when you can't find your rolling pin): I like the French-style pin that's basically just a 18-inch long, wide stick that's slightly tapered on the ends. It doesn't leave ridges in the dough when you roll it out.

Pizza Cutter: It's not just for slicing pizza. This can be used to cut uniform strips of dough, too.

8 to 10-Inch Wire Whisk: Eggs, pastry cream, whipped cream: you name it, I beat it!

Heatproof 9 to 12-inch Rubber Spatula: Another tool for scraping and stirring.

Ice Cream Scoops: Technically, these are called "dishers," and they're often used to scoop out ice cream, but they're also handy for portioning out cookies and muffins so each comes out the same size. I keep several sizes handy, from 1 to 4 ounces.

Microplane Grater: Use this to zest citrus and grate fresh nutmeg.

Metal Spider: This is a wide, shallow skimmer, roughly 5 to 8 inches, essential for frying.

8-Inch Metal Strainer: Use this to drain pasta, canned beans, and dried fruit that's been soaking overnight.

12-Inch Wooden Spoon: Technically, a rubber spatula serves the same purpose, but there's just something romantic about stirring a pot of soup with an old wooden spoon. Also, if you can't find giant chopsticks for flipping your doughnuts in hot oil, the ends of two wooden spoons work perfectly.

Plastic Spray Bottles: I keep one with water for misting loaves of bread while they're rising. I also keep a second one filled with olive oil, which I use for everything from spritzing salad greens and roasted veggies to oiling the top of my focaccia dough or the inside of the tub holding my dough so it doesn't stick.

Docker: This is a roller that is covered in spikes to poke small holes in dough. It allows the dough to rise evenly without any giant air bubbles under the surface. In France, they call this tool a "mother-in-law" because of the grating sound it makes as it moves across the table.

Candy Thermometer: This is ideal for doughnuts. Place it in the oil to make sure it's the proper temperature before frying.

Unscented Kitchen-Sized Garbage Bags: These are great for proofing bread. A sheet pan will slide perfectly inside, or you can keep it flat and cover the rising dough on the table.

Big Stuff That Doesn't Fit in Drawers

Plastic Containers with Lids: I love those made by Cambro, which have become widely available to nonprofessionals through websites such as Amazon and WebstaurantStore. They nest, they have airtight lids, they come in different sizes, and volumetric measures are marked on the sides.

Metal Nesting Bowls: These also come in glass or plastic, but I prefer a metal set because they're light and thin, so they take up less space. I place a metal bowl on top of a pot of boiling water to create a double boiler.

6-Quart Steel Pot: For boiling water.

Steel or Cast-Iron Pot for Frying: This can be the same one you use to boil water, but I prefer a 12-inch-wide, shallower frying pot.

10 to 12-Inch Steel Sauté Pan: I use this to prep veggies for pizzas.

Parchment Paper: This is great for making sure nothing sticks to your sheet pan. You can also fold it into a cone, fill it with buttercream, and pipe designs on doughnuts and cakes.

6 to 8-Quart Dutch Oven: You can bake an amazing loaf of bread in this cast-iron pot with a lid. The lid traps the steam, creating a great crust. It's also great for roasting meats.

Baking Sheets and Pans: I prefer 13 by 18-inch baking sheets with edges and 9 by 13-inch baking pans.

Bottle Opener: Baking makes us thirsty!

If You Want to Splurge

Stand Mixer: You will need this if you plan to cream butter and sugar for cookies or make any of the enriched (loaded-with-butter) doughs in this book. Most mixers come with paddle, whisk, and dough hook attachments. A mixer as small as 4 quarts will work just fine, though if you plan on making "family-size" batches, it might be best to opt for a larger 8-quart model.

Blender or Food Processor: When I first separated from my husband and moved out, the only thing I took from the kitchen was my Vitamix blender that I spent years scrimping and saving to buy. If you have a good blender, you don't really need a food processor, and vice versa. Just pick one or the other, and buy the best one you can afford so you're not replacing it every six months when the motor burns out (or maybe that's just me!).

Stuff You Don't Need

Double Boiler: See Metal Nesting Bowls (page xv).

Citrus Juicer: Just use your hand and a fork to break up the inside of lemons, limes, oranges, etc.

Garlic Press: See Chef's Knife (page xiii).

Pizza Stone: It's nice to have, but you'll probably crack it in half shortly after you buy it, and a sheet pan can serve the same purpose.

Basic Techniques

The following techniques will be repeated over and over throughout this book. You can familiarize yourself with them here and then check back as needed.

Sifting: Recipes often tell you to sift the dry ingredients together. I've found that dumping them in a big bowl, separate from the wet ingredients, and running a whisk through them a few times does the same job with a lot less effort.

Creaming: The key to making great cookies is to properly cream the butter and sugar before moving on through the recipe. Not only does this process aerate the butter but also it creates an emulsion of sorts that will give the cookies or cake doughnuts a smooth texture. Creaming helps the cookies rise properly and spread properly. If you haven't creamed enough, the cookies will spread too thinly.

I suggest using room-temperature butter. But seriously, who remembers to take the butter out to come to room temperature? You can also just cut the butter into small cubes before placing it in the mixing bowl. Fit a stand mixer with a paddle attachment, and turn the mixer on low speed until the cubes of butter start to smooth out and they aren't stuck against the side of the bowl or the paddle. As soon as the butter is smooth, add the sugar. The grainy texture will help to break down the butter. Next, turn the mixer up to medium-high speed and find something else to occupy your time for the next 5 to 8 minutes. When you come back, the butter and sugar should be almost white in color with barely a hint of yellow from the butter. Scrape the sides and bottom of the bowl using a rubber spatula or bench scraper and let the mixer go for another 2 to 3 minutes before you start adding eggs.

Master the creaming method and you will have perfect cookies every time, I promise.

Hand-Mixing Bread Dough: To be clear, hand-mixing dough is NOT the same as kneading dough. Unless the dough has a significant amount of butter, like brioche, or is very dense, like challah, it can be mixed by hand. Ciabatta, sourdough, and pizza dough are perfect for hand-mixing.

Start with a container that has a lid and can be airtight. It should have enough space to hold double the ingredients. Assume that your dough will rise to twice its original size. Pull your sleeves up, remove any rings or watches, and get your hands dirty.

Add the water first, then add the yeast to the water so it starts to dissolve. Add the flour next, and finish with the salt and remaining ingredients, such as oil or honey. Remember: we are NOT kneading the dough. We ARE creating a homogenous mass of dough. This means the water and flour will be fully incorporated but the dough itself will be a little shaggy. You might have some lumps and bumps, but they will work themselves out during the folding process. Once the liquid and flour are combined, do your best to remove the dough stuck to your fingers and close the container. If the dough isn't in an airtight container, the surface will dry out, preventing any rising.

Every 15 to 30 minutes, fold the dough as instructed on page xx. After three folds, wait 30 more minutes before dividing and/or shaping the dough. The whole process shouldn't take more than 2 hours.

Using a Stand Mixer to Mix Bread Dough: Rather than give an exact time to mix the dough through each stage of development, I feel it's important to understand what the dough should look, feel, and sound like. Times will vary based on different mixers, flours, hydration levels, etc.

First, just like in hand-mixing, the ingredients need to be incorporated into a homogenous mass. Fit the stand mixer with a dough hook. Dump everything into the bowl (I start with wet and then add dry) and mix on the lowest speed setting. The ingredients will combine over the next 2 to 4 minutes. You can continue mixing on the lowest speed as long as you'd like, but it's going to take a very long time to mix the dough to completion on this setting. (The good news is that you will not overmix your dough on the lowest setting. If you walk away and forget that it is mixing while you start another activity, it won't harm the dough.)

I recommend next turning up the mixer speed to medium-high. On a KitchenAid mixer that goes from 1 to 10, this would be a 6; on a Hobart that goes from 1 to 3, this would be a 2. I always stay at a medium or medium-high setting on the mixer unless I am whipping cream. The dough will continue to mix at this speed until it's fully developed. Generally, this will take 8 to 12 minutes.

Rather than set a timer, you will begin to be able to recognize when your dough is ready by looking and listening. The dough will start to clean itself off the sides of the bowl and curl up around the dough hook. This is actually called the "cleanup" phase of mixing. You might have to stop the mixer a couple times to remove the dough from the hook so it mixes evenly. The best indication that your dough is done is the sound it will make as it thwacks against the side of the bowl like the beat of a drum. After it has done this for 1 to 2 minutes, mixing is complete.

Once you think your dough is done, you can stop the mixer and pull out a small lump. Gently stretch this lump as wide as you can; you should be able to stretch it thin enough that you can almost see through it. This is called the "window test." If you can do this without ripping the dough, it's done. If it is impossible to pull a window, mix for another minute or two and try again.

When you are finished mixing, remove the dough from the bowl and place it in an airtight container at least twice its size.

Folding: Nearly every bread recipe in this book will ask you to fold the dough. That's because there are two types of development in yeasted doughs.

In the first, chemical development, the yeast gobbles up the natural sugars in the wheat, producing carbon dioxide (bubbles) and alcohol (flavor). The proteins in the flour are denaturing to create bubblegum-like strands of gluten.

The second, mechanical development, happens any time you or the mixer kneads the dough. I don't recommend spending any length of time kneading dough by hand because you will wear yourself out and there's really no need. Time and chemical development will do all of the hard work for you.

You just need to help the dough along with a fold every once in a while. If you're hand-mixing, you should fold the dough every 15 to 30 minutes. If you're using a dough hook and stand mixer, the fold should come later in the process, say, 45 to 60 minutes, or roughly halfway through the bulk fermentation stage (when the dough rises in one giant piece).

In addition to developing the strength of the dough, folding also helps to even out its temperature. Fermentation generates heat, and the core of the dough can become very warm, sometimes too warm, while the outside surface of the dough is the temperature of the room where it's resting (this may be your kitchen; it could also be your refrigerator, depending on the recipe). When you fold the dough, it brings the exterior temperature to the core to neutralize the dough's overall temperature. Remember that as yeast warms up, it becomes more active, so it's best to have consistent temperature and therefore yeast activity throughout the entire mass of dough.

The dough will take on the shape of its container, which in most cases will be rectangular or square. This means the resting dough has four sides. If you use a round bowl to proof your dough, treat the circle as if it's a drop-leaf table and process the same way. To fold the dough, take one side at a time, stretch it out slightly from the mass, and fold it over the center. I fold top, then bottom, then left, then right, but you can go in any order. Every time a recipe states "fold the dough," you need to fold all four sides into the center. Not just two—all four. To finish the fold, turn the dough upside down so that the pieces that were folded over are now resting on the bottom of the container. If you skip this final step, the folds will unravel.

Proofing/Rising: If there's one thing I hate more than anything else I see in a cookbook, it's the dreaded "doubled in size" instruction. How do you know when your bread is "doubled in size"? How can you possibly remember how big it was when you started and whether it's exactly twice as large now? Maybe it spread out a little, so it will never be two times as tall.

Here's a better way: the finger poke test. Gently poke the dough with one finger. You should see an indentation in the surface of the dough. If the indentation stays or completely deflates your dough, it is overproofed. If the indentation immediately springs back so you can barely tell you poked the dough at all, it is underproofed. If the indentation comes back about halfway, it is perfectly proofed and ready to go in the oven (see photo below).

The key to proper proofing is to make sure that your dough stays moist. You can do this by draping a piece of plastic wrap over it. I use unscented kitchen-sized garbage bags because they perfectly cover a 9 by 13-inch sheet pan. If the dough gets a dry crust, it won't be able to rise. If you think your dough is drying out, you can use a spray bottle to mist it with water or reapply egg wash if the recipe calls for it.

Proof in a room that has a moderate temperature, 68° to 72°F. If it's any warmer, the dough will rise faster, and often the outside surface of the dough will rise more quickly than the center. This will create a bunch of big air pockets near the top of your loaf and tiny, dense bubbles on the bottom of your loaf, which you don't want. You want equally sized air bubbles throughout your loaves.

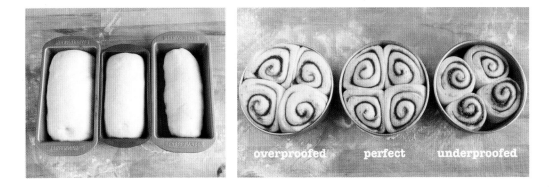

overproofed   perfect   underproofed

Scoring: There is water, or moisture, in every dough we bake. When water is introduced to high heat, it turns to steam. The steam gets trapped inside the loaves of bread by the gluten network. It helps the bread to rise, and it creates beautiful bubbles of air. As the steam builds, it needs a place to go. It's like blowing a bubble with gum: it can get only so big before it pops. When the steam departs from the bread, it chooses the weakest spot on the loaf to break free. In some loaves, like ciabatta, this creates a distinct look to the bread, the breaking point.

I like to have as much control as possible over the entire baking process. One way to control the steam and the breaking point is to score the bread, or cut it, before it goes into the oven. You will need a very sharp serrated knife or, my preferred method, using a straight razor. The razor used for scoring bread is called a lame, pronounced with a soft *a*, the opposite of what my kids think of me when I tell them it's bedtime.

You can go down a rabbit hole of fancy scoring techniques, but the most basic, end-to-end cut will do the trick. The cut should be made at a 45-degree angle. This will give you the "ear" that opens up to let more dough rise through. The bread should be scored immediately before going into the oven. If you let it sit outside the oven after it is cut, all the lovely bubbles you worked so hard to create inside the loaf will start to escape and your loaves will flatten.

How to Make a Sourdough Build: In spring 2020, when the world went into pandemic quarantine, everyone became a baker, and everyone wanted to experiment with sourdough. I have a starter at Montclair Bread Company I've been feeding since May 2012, twice a day, every day. I have an emotional connection to the time I've dedicated to this baby. When my customers started asking whether they could buy sourdough starter from me, I refused. I want bakers, new and old, to have the commitment to feed this thing and watch it grow to feel the same sense of pride when their little babies create beautiful loaves of tangy bread. It's a very personal process.

A viable sourdough starter, one that you can use to make bread rise, can be created in 5 days. It is also known as a "mother," or a "levain." Wild yeast is trapped from the air (yes, it's on every surface, and you didn't even know it!) and captured in the flour and water mixture. Every time you add fresh flour and water to the culture, it is called a feeding. Feeding should occur at the same time each day, as if you are feeding your child or a pet you'd like to keep alive. This process will create waste, but I try to keep it minimal. If you plan to make sourdough daily, you can get creative with your math skills and chart a feeding schedule that is in line with your sourdough production so the only leftover blob is what you will be feeding for the next day's dough. This is how we feed at MBCo.

The flour can be any kind you'd like. I LOVE using whole-grain flour in my sourdough starter. The process softens the bran flakes, which will give you a better rise in your final dough because they won't be cutting into the gluten strands you're working hard to build.

If you keep only one sourdough starter on hand, which I recommend because you'll drive yourself crazy trying to keep up feeding a whole litter of levains, feed it with white flour. When you're ready to build for your recipe, start the feedings with the flour of your choice. By day 5, you'll have converted the culture over to the new flour.

Your starter can be kept dormant in the fridge until you are ready to start feeding it for a new adventure. It may get a pinkish-gray film on top, which you can skim off and continue as planned. Yeast is a fungus you are cultivating, so don't get freaked out if it displays characteristics of food you would typically throw away. If your sourdough starter smells like a cross between a gym locker and a brewery, you are doing it right.

Here's my tried-and-true formula:

Day 1: Mix ¼ cup flour and ¼ cup water.

Day 2: Mix ½ cup starter (from day 1) with ½ cup flour and ½ cup water.

Day 3: Mix ½ cup starter (from day 2, discarding the leftover) with ½ cup flour and ½ cup water.

Day 4: Mix ½ cup starter (from day 3, discarding the leftover) with ½ cup flour and ½ cup water.

Day 5: Mix 1½ cups starter (from day 4) with 1½ cups flour and 1½ cups water.

When the starter is mature and ready to make dough rise, it will have big, pronounced bubbles floating on top, and it will smell like a funky locker room.

CHILDHOOD FAVORITES

From the beginning, the only thing I cared about in life—and the only thing I was ever good at—was baking.

Age 3: My grandmother, Mom-Mom (later called Mombo), taught me how to write my name with a piping bag full of buttercream on a flimsy paper plate and how to pipe roses on pastry nails, which I licked off before starting again. I didn't yet know how to hold a pencil, but she had priorities. During my childhood deep in the rural farm country along the Chesapeake Bay in Maryland, she was the main grown-up in my life; my parents divorced before I was a year old, and both worked long hours at work, school, and my father's convenience store.

Age 8: I tried to bake brownies on my own while my grandparents were outside mowing the lawn. I pulled out the *Better Homes and Gardens Cookbook* with the red gingham cover and flipped to the page already stained with melted butter from my previous brownie bakes with Mom-Mom. I managed to turn on the stovetop and melt the baker's chocolate squares with butter until they formed a thin liquid. I used a paper towel and Crisco to grease the square pan just like I watched my grandmother do hundreds of times before.

Before I could add the dry ingredients to the mix, I started to smell something burning. I had remembered to preheat the oven, but I forgot to remove the big plastic tub of sandwich breads and rolls my grandmother stored inside. By the time I ran outside to get my grandparents' attention, flames engulfed the small brown oven, and melted plastic dripped onto the electric heating elements.

My grandmother didn't think twice: she grabbed a box of baking soda from the cabinet, opened the oven door, and dumped baking soda on top of the flames. The fire was extinguished in seconds, but I was left crying and shaking with fright.

My grandmother looked me in the eyes and said, "Now I can finally get that new oven. I've wanted to replace this one for years."

And my grandfather, Pop, added: "Well, Jitterbug, that's why pencils have erasers."

Age 13: My other grandfather, Pop-Pop John, was not a fan of children. When I was 8 and my cousin was born, my grandfather announced, "I'm over this 'Pop-Pop,' 'Poppy' shit. The kid can call me 'Sir' until he's old enough to call me 'John.'" From that point on, I was the only one who called him Pop-Pop. The rest of the family called him Sir.

Mom-Mom taught me how to bake, but John taught me how to run a business. "If you're on time, you're late. Always bring a paper to read before the meeting starts."

John talked to me like I was an adult. Whenever I stayed with him, both of us woke up with the sun. He made coffee that wasn't Folgers. Then we walked into town, where he introduced me to the coffee shop that made the best muffins or a bakery with exceptional croissants. At lunchtime, he took me to the bistro he had discovered that had only six tables but made the best gazpacho.

Each summer he and my grandmother Jackie took me on a road trip that was my only chance all year to leave the Delmarva Peninsula. We went to Montreal, stopping in Boston and Burlington. We went to Gainesville, Florida, stopping in Richmond, Charleston, and St. Augustine. We went to their house in Martha's Vineyard, ate breakfast at the Black Dog Café, and sat on a park bench by the waterfront. John read the *Wall Street Journal* while I filled out the *New York Times* crossword puzzle.

Years later, our worlds collided when the *Wall Street Journal* started a food section. Occasionally, I'd get an envelope in the mail, with no note attached. Just a column that John thought would interest me.

Age 14: I arrived to work at the Ironstone Cafe in Chestertown, Maryland, 30 minutes early. The last busser to arrive had to vacuum the carpet in the dining room. It would not be me. I sat at a table and polished trays of silverware with vodka to make them shine and then tucked them into the stacks of napkins I had folded minutes before. I had just been promoted to expeditor. In some kitchens, this is the highest position one can hold, often reserved for the actual chef. In this kitchen, run by Chef Kevin, it was a step slightly above the dishwasher. My job was to hoist the giant tray of meals on my shoulder, take it through the swinging door to the dining room, and deliver it to the proper diners at the proper table, making sure to pass the plate in front of them from right to left and never left to right. If I made one mistake, Barbara, the front of the house manager and Chef Kevin's wife, would notice, pull me into a corner, and sternly scold me in a very low, very frightening Maleficent kind of voice. I spent most nights trembling in fear, nervous I would make another mistake. No matter how hard I tried, I couldn't make it through a night without fucking something up.

Tonight, Chef Kevin was screaming at me. "Where did those plates go? Table 11? They were supposed to go to Table 13? NO, you can't take the food away; we have to make it again. Now we're behind on the rest of the tickets. How hard is it to get it right??? Are you stupid?"

I fought to hold back the tears welling up in my eyes as he threw a plate on the ground just to hear the crash when it shattered. At least one plate went down during every service. I hung my head low, trying not to make eye contact with anyone, afraid the pools of water in my eyes would be visible.

I picked up the next tray, the next, and the next, serving the crab cakes, barbecue ribs, and the sweetbreads Chef Kevin was famous for. I didn't say a word to anyone. When I brought a stack of dirty dishes back into the kitchen, Norma Jean, the dishwasher, whispered to me, "It's okay, baby; he just likes to hear himself yell. You're doin' great." That's when I realized the most important person in any kitchen, the one who truly holds it together, is not the one with the starched white color. It is the one with the mucky apron washing every plate, every fork, and every bus tub.

After two years bussing tables at the Ironstone Cafe and the Kennedyville Inn, Kevin and Barbara's second restaurant, I took a job as a hostess at a local marina, the Great Oak Restaurant and Lodge. I got to wear dresses, and I didn't have to duck plates flying across the kitchen. The restaurant had nearly eighty tables. On a busy night, I had to manage seating sections for twelve servers with a two-hour wait for a table. I got used to having my ass grabbed by gropey old boaters and being slipped twenty-dollar bills in an effort to move to the top of the list. I was the youngest on the staff, but my maturity allowed me to pass for older than I actually was. Bottles of Malibu Rum and Southern Comfort were consumed throughout the night.

I grew up fast, way too fast.

Age 17: I graduated from high school a year early and cashed in the money I made working in restaurants to spend a year studying in Lamballe, northern France. There, I assimilated into life and culture on a small pig farm, attending classes in economics at a lycée during the day. This was my first time spending more than two nights in the same bed with a family that was still intact. I was comforted by the consistency.

I had grown up feasting on all that the Chesapeake Bay had to offer, but that was nothing compared to what I found in Lamballe. My first meal at the family table started with thin carrot soup adorned with tapioca pearls. Next we ate boiled salted potatoes and a sausage I'd never tried before. It certainly wasn't the summer sausage from the Pepperidge Farm holiday box I grew up with. I couldn't quite identify the meat. It was speckled with whole roasted hazelnuts, a truly unique combination. I looked up at my new family after the first bite as they were all watching me to see my reaction. "*Je l'aime beaucoup!*" I said: "I love them very much!"

After which Maman cheered with delight, *"Ça me fait plaisir—it is from our pigs."* I gulped. Somehow I had easily been able to disconnect from the venison my dad hunted and all those pesky crabs we killed in Maryland, but thinking of the pigs across the dirt road from the house ending up on my plate now was a shock to my system.

It was only the beginning of my exposure to what farm-to-table was all about, long before the movement took hold in the United States. I picked out the rabbit from the cages stacked by the pig pens at the farm that would make its way to the dinner table later in the week. Each night, I walked to the farm to fetch a pail of fresh milk from the cows for breakfast the next day. In the morning, the milk was boiled and poured into small bowls, topped off with chicory-infused coffee used for dunking toasted slices of baguette.

I stood in the garage watching Mamie, my French grandmother, make endless amounts of traditional Breton buckwheat crepes called galettes. Once she flipped the giant disc, she cracked an egg, fresh from the chicken coop beside my bedroom window, right onto the center of the crepe and spread it around. She quickly sprinkled shredded Emmentaler cheese over the egg and placed a thick slice of ham dead center. As the egg and cheese began to bubble from the heat of the cast-iron plate under the crepe, she quickly folded it into a triangle, plopped it in a bowl, and poured *lait ribot*, fermented French buttermilk, over the top. I devoured mine and went for seconds.

Age 19: Bored with my classes at the University of Florida, I sat in lecture halls packed with 300 students, largely ignoring the professors in order to read a stack of culinary magazines. In order to pay the rent, I launched a baking business, selling cowboy cookies and rocky road brownies to local coffee shops and a sandwich shack called Steamers that was run by the low-key cofounder of the Flying Dog Brewery.

I loved working in the restaurant industry, but not because of the food. It was about the culture I found. I lived in a warehouse with makeshift walls and frequented punk rock shows with my roommates, who were all musicians and restaurant employees. My roommates and I hosted concerts in our house, then drew straws to see who had to borrow the mop bucket from their employer so we could clean up the spilled beer and cigarette butts.

In that warehouse, I began reading Anthony Bourdain's landmark restaurant book, *Kitchen Confidential*, and George Orwell's memoir, *Down and Out in Paris and London*. After reading Bourdain's stories about feeding the "mother dough" and the calm retreat he found in the pastry kitchen, I left behind the fast-paced grill station job I was working and began baking at a vegan café inside a used bookstore. Like Bourdain, I found serenity at 2 a.m. in the kitchen.

MOMBO'S CARROT CAKE

I never wanted to make cakes at Montclair Bread because they required more attention than I wanted to give any one menu item. But I have a weakness for my grandmother Mombo's carrot cake. It's perfect: simple, no frills, no extras like raisins or pineapple to take away from the sweet carrots. It was actually a recipe passed down from my great-grandmother, Ruth, who was the head cook for a one-room schoolhouse full of children.

My friends were so thrilled every time I made the cake for a party or barbecue that I finally caved and put Mombo's carrot cake on the menu at Montclair Bread. I will never forget the last conversation I had with Mombo before she succumbed to a brutal fight with bone cancer. "I can't make enough of it. It's selling out every day," I told her.

"Why would anyone pay money for that carrot cake?" she replied. "It's just something we make at home. It's not fancy enough for a bakery."

Clearly, my customers disagree.

Cake
2 cups sugar

1½ cups vegetable oil

4 large eggs

1 teaspoon vanilla extract

3 cups finely grated carrots (about 2 carrots)

2 cups all-purpose flour

1 ½ teaspoons baking soda

2 teaspoons ground cinnamon

Frosting
8 ounces cream cheese, at room temperature

1 cup (2 sticks) unsalted butter, at room temperature

1 teaspoon vanilla extract

3½ cups (1 pound) confectioners' sugar

2 cups crushed walnuts, for garnish

Preheat the oven to 350°F. Grease the sides and bottoms of two 8-inch cake pans with canola oil and dust with flour.

To make the cake, stir together the sugar, vegetable oil, eggs, and vanilla in a large bowl, using a wooden spoon, until smooth. Fold in the carrots. Stir in the flour, baking soda, and cinnamon. The batter will be wet. Don't worry—you didn't do anything wrong!

continued

Divide the batter between the two cake pans. Bake for about 35 minutes, or until a toothpick inserted in the center comes out clean.

While the cakes are cooling, make the frosting. In the bowl of a stand mixer fitted with a paddle attachment, beat the cream cheese and butter on high speed until it is light, fluffy, and nearly white in color. This should take 5 to 8 minutes. Add the vanilla and beat until it is fully incorporated. Decrease the mixer to low speed. Add the confectioners' sugar ½ cup at a time, until incorporated. Return the mixer to high speed and beat until light and fluffy.

To assemble the cake, first make sure the layers are completely cooled; otherwise, the frosting will melt, and the layers will slide off each other. Wait for an additional 20 minutes after you think your cake is completely cool, if you are super impatient about these things. You don't want all your hard work to go to waste if you jump the gun and frost a warm cake! The cake layers can also be made a day ahead. They should be wrapped tightly in plastic wrap and kept at room temperature.

To maximize the cake-to-frosting ratio, you can cut each of the 8-inch layers in half horizontally using a serrated bread knife, to create four cake layers in total. If you are nervous about taking this step, using two layers is just fine.

Using a spatula, spread an even layer of frosting on top of the first layer, carefully going all the way out to the edge. Stack the next layer on top and repeat until all the layers, including the final layer, are covered in frosting. Use the spatula to spread frosting around the sides. If you're feeling nutty, press chopped walnuts into the sides of the frosted cake. This also helps to cover up any shortcomings you may have when it comes to frosting a cake. The cake is best served at room temperature, but it can be carefully wrapped with plastic wrap against the cut side and refrigerated for up to 5 days.

STRAWBERRY CAKE

Makes one 8-inch layer cake, serves 8 to 10

When it came to birthdays, I was as spoiled as they come. Having a grandmother who is a talented cake baker—and who lets you believe you are the center of the universe—has its perks. For my fifth birthday, I asked for a strawberry wedding cake with three tiers. I also asked for a Cabbage Patch doll. I invited my entire kindergarten class to have cake with me in my backyard. This was long before it was considered mandatory to invite the whole class. Mombo made the perfect cake, with all the tiers, made taller by long plastic columns separating the layers. The white cake was adorned with little pink buttercream flowers and pink buttercream ribbons. I also got the doll of my dreams.

Twenty years later, Mombo helped me make my actual wedding cake, the same strawberry cake, this time with cream cheese frosting and bouquets of multicolored fresh Gerbera daisies adorning the layers.

I've eaten cakes and desserts all over the world, many made by celebrated chefs at critically acclaimed restaurants and bakeries. At Montclair Bread Company, I make every cake from scratch. But this simple strawberry cake, made from a box with a little extra love, is my absolute favorite thing on the planet. It's the reason I bake my own birthday cake every year. Comfort and joy, sitting on my plate.

Flour, for dusting the pans

1 cup water

¾ cup vegetable oil

4 large eggs

1 box strawberry cake mix (any brand works fine)

1 (3-ounce) box vanilla Cook & Serve pudding mix

1 (2.6-ounce) package Dream Whip whipped topping mix (usually available in the pudding aisle)

1 recipe Cream Cheese Frosting (page 114)
Fresh strawberries, for topping (optional)

Preheat the oven to 350°F. Grease two 8-inch cake pans with vegetable oil and dust with flour.

Whisk together the water, vegetable oil, and eggs in a large bowl. Stir in the cake mix, pudding mix, and Dream Whip. Whisk until smooth. Divide the batter evenly between the two cake pans. Bake for 30 to 40 minutes, until a toothpick inserted in the center comes out clean.

To assemble the cake, first make sure the layers are completely cooled; otherwise, the frosting will melt, and the layers will slide off each other. Wait for an additional 20 minutes after you think your cake is completely cool, if you are super impatient about these things. You don't want all your hard work to go to waste if you jump the gun and frost a warm cake! The cake layers can also be made a day ahead. They should be wrapped tightly in plastic wrap and kept at room temperature.

Using a spatula, spread an even layer of frosting on top of the first layer, carefully going all the way out to the edge. Stack the next layer on top and repeat until all the layers, including the final layer, are

covered in frosting. Use the spatula to spread frosting around the sides. If you want to be extra fancy, you can place fresh strawberries on top of the cake. Slice them up into a fun arrangement or simply leave them whole, it's up to you. The cake is best served at room temperature, but it can be carefully wrapped with plastic wrap against the cut side and refrigerated for up to 5 days.

MOMBO'S BREAD PUDDING

Serves 8 to 12

Mombo taught me most of what I know about baking, except for bread. She did know how to use bread in other recipes, though: this dessert was one of my Pop's favorites. Don't know what to do with all that bread you bought that's staling on your counter? How about the milk that has only a day left before it expires? This is the answer to both.

6 cups bread, cut into 1-inch cubes (anything goes: baguettes, doughnuts, croissants, whole grain, cinnamon raisin)

2 apples, any variety, peeled and thinly sliced, or 1 cup chocolate chips, dried fruit, or nuts

3 cups milk of your choice

6 large eggs

1 tablespoon vanilla extract

½ cup sugar

1 tablespoon ground cinnamon

¼ teaspoon ground nutmeg

Whipped cream, Cool Whip, or vanilla ice cream, for serving (optional)

Preheat the oven to 350°F. Spray a 9 by 13-inch pan with cooking spray.

Toss the bread and apples (or chocolate or other fruit, if using) together in the pan.

In a medium bowl, whisk together the milk, eggs, vanilla, sugar, cinnamon, and nutmeg. Pour the mixture over the bread and apples. Use your hands to squish the bread mixture together and break it down a bit more. Let the pudding sit at room temperature for 5 to 10 minutes so it fully absorbs the milk and eggs.

Bake for about 45 minutes, or until the top is deep brown and the center is no longer jiggly when you jostle the pan.

Serve warm, with whipped cream or ice cream, if desired. This will keep wrapped airtight in the fridge for up to 5 days—it is good cold, too.

CHOCOLATE MAYONNAISE CAKE

Makes one single 8-inch cake, serves 8 to 10

Before you say "ew, gross," let's think about this. When you break it down, mayo is just shelf-stable eggs, oil, and vinegar . . . the same ingredients you need to bake a yummy, moist cake.

This was a recipe from my great-aunt Naomi. We called her "Aunt Nelma" because that's what "Naomi" sounded like when my mother tried to say it as a little girl. Naomi Wheat was an English teacher in Galena, Maryland, for forty years. She lived to be 100 years old. Her love for word puzzles and grammar never waned. It's no wonder her cake holds a special place in my heart.

1 cup mayonnaise

1 cup granulated sugar

2 cups all-purpose flour

¼ cup dark cocoa powder

1 teaspoon baking soda

Pinch of table salt

1 cup hot tap water, divided

1 teaspoon vanilla extract

Confectioners' sugar, for topping

Frosting, whipped cream, or fresh berries, for topping (optional)

Preheat the oven to 350°F. Grease one 8-inch cake pan with canola oil and dust with flour.

In a large bowl, whisk the mayonnaise and sugar together.

In a separate medium bowl, stir together the flour, cocoa powder, baking soda, and salt.

Gradually add one third of the flour mixture, then ⅓ cup of the hot water with the vanilla to the mayonnaise mixture, alternating back and forth in thirds, whisking between additions until the batter is smooth and incorporated. Pour the batter into the pan and bake for 30 to 40 minutes, until a knife or toothpick inserted in the center of the cake comes out clean.

When the cake is cool, dust with the confectioners' sugar. Or you can top with your favorite frosting or finish with whipped cream and fresh berries, if desired. The cake is best served at room temperature, but it can be carefully wrapped with plastic wrap and stored at room temperature for up to 5 days.

APPLE DUMPLINGS

Mombo's apple dumplings were worth waiting all year for. She made them only during the fall apple season, when she or a neighbor could pick the apples from the farm. They had to be just the right size, as big as a tennis ball, and just the right kind, Gala or McIntosh. Looking back, I'm not sure whether she waited for the perfect apples because they were worth waiting for or just because this recipe can be a real pain in the ass.

Apple dumplings created a divide in our family. Some of us, myself included, believed the warm vanilla cream to be a requirement. Others felt that the cream ruined a perfectly good dumpling, rendering it too soggy to eat.

After my grandmother passed away, my aunt was frantically searching for her apple dumpling recipe. "But how do you make the sauce in the bottom of the pan?" She didn't believe me when I told her it didn't exist: the sauce just makes itself! The combination of cinnamon, sugar, butter, and apple goo creates a caramel-like sauce that is so heavenly. I eat the top of the dumpling first, saving the last, saucy, soggy bite for last!

Dumplings

2 cups sugar

2 tablespoons ground cinnamon

6 medium apples (such as Gala, McIntosh, or Honeycrisp)

1 recipe Pie Dough (page 28)

½ cup (1 stick) unsalted butter, divided, at room temperature

1 cup water

Vanilla Cream

2 cups cold whole milk

½ cup sugar

1 teaspoon vanilla extract

1 tablespoon cornstarch

Preheat the oven to 350°F.

To make the dumplings, stir the sugar and cinnamon together in a small bowl.

Peel the apples, then core them—try to leave them intact, but you can cut them in half lengthwise to remove their cores, if necessary. Divide the pie dough into eight equal pieces. Cut the butter into ¼-inch-thick slices.

continued

Use a rolling pin to roll out each piece of dough into a 5-inch circle about ¼ inch thick. Place an apple in the center of each circle. Spoon ¼ cup of the cinnamon-sugar mixture on top of each apple and into the core. Top each apple with one slice of butter, reserving the rest. Wrap the pie dough around each apple and press it together into the top of the core so that the apple is completely covered in dough. Repeat with the remaining dough and apples.

Arrange the dough-wrapped apples in a 9 by 13-inch roasting pan. They can touch each other. Sprinkle any remaining cinnamon-sugar mixture over the tops of the dough-wrapped apples. Top with the remaining butter slices. Pour the water into the bottom of the pan. Cover the pan tightly with aluminum foil. Bake for 45 minutes. Remove the foil and bake for an additional 15 minutes, or until the tops of the apples start to brown and the sugar starts to caramelize.

Remove the dumplings from the oven. They can be served hot, but it's best to let them cool to a non–molten sugar level to avoid blistering the roof of your mouth.

While they are cooling, make the vanilla cream. Continuously whisk the milk, sugar, vanilla, and cornstarch together in a small saucepan over medium heat, until the mixture starts to bubble. Keep whisking for 1 minute more until the sauce thickens. Remove the cream from the heat and let it cool. (You can also do as Mombo did: combine all of the ingredients in a 4-cup microwave-safe pitcher or bowl and microwave in 1-minute increments, stirring between each one, until thickened, 3 to 4 minutes.)

I like to put my dumpling in a bowl and LIBERALLY pour the cream over the top so it puddles around the sides. The apple dumplings can also be served with vanilla ice cream. They are especially yummy eaten straight from the refrigerator for breakfast the next morning! The cream and dumplings will keep wrapped airtight in the fridge for up to 4 days.

EASTER EGGS

I rarely saw Mombo making these candy Easter eggs every year. She tried her best to do it when no one was around so she could hide them from my grandfather, who would eat them all before Easter if he knew their whereabouts. Though I don't know whether that's even possible, because she made HUNDREDS of these things. Sometimes they were under the bed in the guest room, and other years, they were stashed in the basement. I would start looking for them weeks before Easter so I could lay claim to all the peanut butter eggs.

These are really sweet, like nothing-but-sugar sweet. Just warning you. There is nothing classy about this recipe. My grandma used shortening, but I upgraded to butter. These are simple, approachable, and fun to make with kids.

½ cup (1 stick) unsalted butter, at room temperature

3½ cups (1 pound) confectioners' sugar

½ cup coconut flakes, peanut butter, maraschino cherries, or flavor bits of your choice

3 to 5 teaspoons whole milk

2 cups (12 ounces) semisweet chocolate, coarsely chopped or chips

1 tablespoon coconut oil or other oil of your choice

Frosting, flowers, sprinkles, or other baking decorations (optional)

In the bowl of a stand mixer fitted with a paddle attachment, cream the butter, confectioners' sugar, and coconut flakes or other flavoring of choice on medium speed. Add the milk, 1 teaspoon at a time, and mix until incorporated. Wait for the milk to fully incorporate before adding the next teaspoon. Stop adding milk when the dough resembles Play-Doh. If you overdo it, the dough will liquify.

Roll tablespoonfuls of dough and shape them into eggs. Place the eggs on a baking sheet; cover with plastic wrap and refrigerate for at least 2 hours or overnight.

continued

When the eggs are chilled, create a double boiler by pouring a few inches of water into a saucepan, then setting a heatproof bowl on top. (The bowl should completely cover the top of the pot so steam builds underneath.) Heat the saucepan over medium heat, bringing the water to a boil. Decrease the heat to low and let simmer. Add the chocolate and oil to the bowl and stir together until melted and smooth.

Line a baking sheet with parchment paper. Using the tip of a paring knife, pick up each egg and dip it into the chocolate. Place the chocolate-covered egg, carefully, onto the baking sheet. Decorate immediately with frosting flowers or edible sprinkles, if desired, or just leave the eggs plain.

The eggs will keep wrapped airtight at room temperature for up to 2 weeks.

COWBOY COOKIES

When I was a freshman in college at the University of Florida, I had a hard time paying attention to my professors. Instead, I read *Bon Appétit* and *Gourmet* magazines. One day, I found a recipe for cowboy cookies. I went home from class and baked a batch that day, swapping walnuts for the local pecans and making the recipe vegan to suit my diet at the time. The cookies became so popular with my friends that I decided to try to sell them to local coffee shops and lunch dives. Before long, I couldn't keep up with cowboy cookie production in my tiny oven. A line of people greeted my weekly delivery at one popular lunch spot, Steamers, where the owner, Art, labeled them "Rachel's Treats."

A local vegetarian joint, the Book Lover's Café, caught wind of my treats and offered me my very first baking job. Many nights I would leave the bar at last call and go straight to the café to start baking. I've modified the recipe over the years, adding cloves and cinnamon to evoke Mexican chocolate, adding raisins and pumpkin seeds, and proudly using butter instead of my former vegan substitute. I've now sold them in several states, becoming a hit beyond Montclair Bread Co.

1 cup (2 sticks) unsalted butter, at room temperature
¾ cup granulated sugar
¾ cup dark brown sugar
2 large eggs
1 teaspoon vanilla extract
2 cups all-purpose flour
2 cups rolled oats
1 teaspoon baking soda

½ teaspoon baking powder
½ teaspoon kosher salt
1 teaspoon ground cinnamon
¼ teaspoon ground cloves
1 cup bittersweet chocolate chips or chunks
¾ cup chopped pecans
¾ cup raisins
¼ cup pumpkin seeds

In the bowl of a stand mixer fitted with a paddle attachment, cream the butter and sugars on medium-high speed, until light, fluffy, and white in color, about 5 to 8 minutes. As it aerates, the butter becomes less yellow. If it is still bright yellow, continue beating it. I like to start the creaming process while I'm still gathering the rest of my ingredients so my impatience doesn't get the best of me.

continued

continued from page 19

Add the eggs and vanilla, and beat until the mixture becomes smooth. Stir in the flour, oats, baking soda, baking powder, salt, cinnamon, and cloves, until just combined. Add the chocolate chips, pecans, raisins, and pumpkin seeds, and stir until incorporated.

Scoop into tablespoon-sized balls. Place them on a cookie sheet; refrigerate 10 to 15 minutes.

Preheat the oven to 350°F. Line two baking sheets with parchment paper.

Flatten the chilled balls into ½-inch-thick rounds and arrange them on a baking sheet, 2 inches apart. Bake for 10 to 12 minutes, until the edges of the cookies start to brown. Remove them from the tray with a spatula and cool them on a rack or wooden cutting board. They will keep wrapped airtight at room temperature for up to 2 weeks.

PEACH BLUEBERRY BUCKLE

Serves 12

Summers at Mombo's house meant running barefoot across the hot blacktop as fast as I could to avoid blistering the bottoms of my feet. This also meant eating Schwan's ice cream sandwiches in the small aboveground pool so I wouldn't "make a mess of the blacktop," as my grandmother would say. I'd occasionally hear the whirring of the old ice cream maker in the garage, filled with ice and rock salt churning the most perfect vanilla ice cream I've ever tasted. Above all, summers were for peaches from Pop's peach tree. Small but mighty, it grew next to Mombo's fish pond. That tiny tree produced bushels of peaches every summer. I couldn't wait for them to ripen. When they were finally ready, we ate peach everything . . . peach ice cream, peach pie, peach preserves, and my favorite, peach buckle. I can't eat a peach without thinking about Pop's tree.

This recipe is another great use for fruit you're looking to repurpose. Go as crazy as you'd like with how the fruit is arranged. I prefer a more rustic look, while my daughter, Josie, likes to prepare hers for exhibition at the Museum of Modern Art.

¼ cup (½ stick) unsalted butter, melted
¾ cup sugar
1 large egg
½ cup whole milk
2 cups all-purpose flour
2 teaspoons baking powder
½ teaspoon table salt
2 peeled and sliced peaches
½ pint fresh blueberries

Topping
1 cup sugar
⅔ cup all-purpose flour
1 teaspoon ground cinnamon
½ cup (1 stick) unsalted butter, melted

Preheat the oven to 350°F. Grease a 9 by 13-inch pan or baking sheet with melted butter.

Stir together the butter, sugar, eggs, and milk. Add the flour, baking powder, and salt; mix until the batter is thick and pasty.

Press the batter into the prepared pan or baking sheet. Top with the peaches and blueberries, gently pressing the fruit into the batter with your hands.

To make the topping, mix together the sugar, flour, cinnamon, and butter. Crumble the topping over the fruit. Make sure to sprinkle it all the way to the edges so every bite of buckle will have a tasty crunch.

Bake for 30 to 45 minutes, until the edges just start to brown and pull away from the sides of the pan and a toothpick inserted in the center comes out clean. Cut the buckle into squares and serve it warm or at room temperature. It's great with a little whipped cream or vanilla ice cream on top. The buckle will keep wrapped airtight at room temperature for up to 4 days.

YOGURT CAKE (*GÂTEAU AU YAOURT*)

Makes 2 loaves, two 8-inch cakes, or 8 mini loaf pans, serves 8 to 10

When I lived in France, my family taught me how to make this cake, the first recipe many French children learn to make because of its simplicity. The texture is similar to pound cake. It's a perfect teatime treat—not too sweet. The olive oil makes it extra special.

The measuring device makes this recipe unique and the perfect first baking adventure. Try to find a six-pack of yogurts that snap apart or single yogurts of similar size. Empty the yogurt out of the container or "pot" and use the pot as your measuring cup for the remaining ingredients. No need for actual cup measures!

2 (6-oz) containers or "pots" of yogurt, plain or vanilla (not Greek)

1 pot olive oil

3 pots sugar

1 teaspoon vanilla extract

3 large eggs

4½ pots all-purpose flour

1 teaspoon baking powder

Preheat the oven to 350°F. Grease two standard loaf pans, two 8-inch cake pans, or 8 mini loaf pans with olive oil.

In a large bowl, empty the yogurt from the containers. Use the empty containers, or "pots," to measure the olive oil and sugar, adding them to the bowl with the yogurt. Add the vanilla and eggs and whisk until the batter is smooth. Add the flour and baking powder to the bowl. Stir the batter until all of the ingredients are combined and it is free of lumps.

Pour the batter into the prepared pans and bake for 30 to 45 minutes for standard loaf pans and cake pans or 20 to 25 minutes for mini loaf pans, until a toothpick inserted into the center of the cake comes out clean. The cakes will keep wrapped airtight at room temperature for up to 3 days.

SHEET PAN BROWNIES

Makes 16 to 24 brownies

I promise this is THE BEST fudge-y brownie recipe EVER.

I adapted this recipe from one that I found printed on the side of a King Arthur Flour bag, circa 2008, when I was living in Milford, Pennsylvania. Since then, I've tried a million others, but I keep coming back to this one.

I use whole wheat flour; you can use all-purpose, too, but if you use wheat, you can tell yourself these are "healthy" brownies because whole grains are good for you.

Most importantly: YOU HAVE TO FOLLOW THE DIRECTIONS! If you want your brownies to be fudge-y and get a perfect sheen on the surface when they come out of the oven, don't skip any of the steps. If you follow the directions, they will be amazing! Simple, right? Nope. This is the official Montclair Bread Co. brownie, which means it's been made (and remade) by many a culinary school intern. I've witnessed more than a few disasters.

1 cup (2 sticks) unsalted butter (or use salted butter and omit the salt)

2 cups sugar

1¼ cups cocoa powder, the darker the better (I like Valrhona)

4 large eggs

1 tablespoon vanilla extract

1 tablespoon strong brewed coffee or espresso

1½ cups whole wheat flour

1 teaspoon kosher salt

1 teaspoon baking powder

2 cups semisweet chocolate chips

Preheat the oven to 350°F. Grease a 9 by 13-inch baking sheet with butter.

Heat the butter and sugar in a small saucepan over low heat, stirring occasionally, just until they form a smooth blend, even if the sugar isn't completely melted. You don't want the mixture to bubble. Remove from the heat.

In a large bowl, whisk together the cocoa powder, eggs, vanilla, and coffee. The mixture will be thick and pasty.

Pour the melted butter and sugar into the bowl with the cocoa mix and whisk together, until smooth and shiny. This is your opportunity to get the lumps out, so beat it until they're gone.

Add the flour, salt, and baking powder. Using a wooden spoon or spatula, stir until the ingredients are just combined. Do not overmix the batter; the brownies will become chewy (not in a good way).

Stir in the chocolate chips. If they melt a little, it's okay. That helps with the fudge-y part.

Pour the batter into the prepared pan and bake for 20 to 24 minutes, just until set. When the brownies are done, the edges should start to pull away a little from the sides of the pan, and the batter shouldn't be jiggly if you jostle the pan. You can't use the toothpick test on brownies, and you don't want to overbake them or the edges will be rock-hard.

If you want the brownies to keep their shape, allow them to cool completely before cutting. If you like to eat warm brownies that might fall apart when you pick them up, then go for it! Brownies will keep wrapped airtight at room temperature for up to 5 days.

PIE DOUGH

Once you master this versatile recipe, the hits will keep coming! In this book alone, you can use this recipe to make Pop Tarts (pages 30 and 33), Hand Pies (page 35), and Apple Dumplings (page 13). You can also use it to make a traditional pie shell or a simple rustic tart.

3½ cups all-purpose flour

1 tablespoon sugar

¼ teaspoon kosher salt

1 cup (2 sticks) very cold unsalted butter (or use salted butter and omit the additional salt), cut into ¼-inch cubes

½ cup tap water, cold

In a large mixing bowl, mix the flour, sugar, and salt together. Add the small cubes of butter. Squish the butter between your fingers to flatten it out. When the butter is flat, add the water and incorporate it into the dough using your hands, until you can work the dough into a ball, with some butter chunks intact. Divide into two smaller balls and flatten into discs. The dough can be rolled out right away or wrapped airtight in plastic wrap and refrigerated for up to 3 days.

When ready to use the dough, roll the disc out on a floured work surface into a rectangular shape about ¼ inch thick: Start in the center and work your way to the edges. Turn the dough 45 degrees and work from different directions (this will prevent it from shrinking when it bakes). Roll the dough as thinly as you can without tearing it, getting the dough as close to ¼ inch thick as possible. Carefully transfer the pie crust to your pie pan and trim the edges as desired. Once the pie shells are complete, they can be wrapped tightly in plastic prior to baking or frozen until you are ready to use them.

STRAWBERRY POP TARTS

Makes 8 to 12 pop tarts

When Josie was born, I was so eager to be a good mom and provide nothing but the healthiest foods to nourish my little girl. I made all of her baby food myself. She never ate a single processed food or knew what soda was, that is, until she went to visit her great grandmother. Mombo's house was a fully stocked wonderland of sugary treats, including the coveted box of strawberry Pop-Tarts. I ignored the tiny voice begging me to buy some for our house during our trips to the grocery store and I set out to make my own less-processed version, which quickly became a fan favorite on the Montclair Bread Co. menu.

1 recipe Pie Dough (page 28)
½ cup strawberry jam

Strawberry Glaze
2 cups confectioners' sugar
¼ cup strawberry jam
1 to 3 tablespoons warm tap water

Preheat the oven to 350°F. Lightly grease a baking sheet with canola oil or line with parchment paper.

To make the pop tarts, roll out the pie dough into a ¼-inch-thick rectangle. Using a pizza cutter and a straight edge, cut the dough into even rectangles about 3 by 5 inches.

Spread 1 teaspoon of the jam in the center of a dough rectangle, leaving ¼ inch of empty space around the edges. Place another rectangle of dough on top to sandwich the filling in the middle. Use a fork to press a seam all the way around the edges and to pierce holes on the top of the tart to vent air during baking.

Place the tarts 1 inch apart on the prepared baking sheet. Bake for 15 to 20 minutes, until light golden brown.

Immediately remove them from the baking sheet and place on a rack to cool completely.

To make the strawberry glaze, whisk together the confectioners' sugar, jam, and 1 tablespoon of the water into a thick paste. Add another tablespoon of water and whisk into a spreadable glaze, adding 1 teaspoon more of water, if necessary. (Adding the water gradually helps smooth out any lumps of sugar.) Drizzle the glaze over the cooled pop tarts. Tarts will keep wrapped airtight at room temperature for up to 3 days.

CINNAMON-BROWN SUGAR POP TARTS

Mombo didn't just stock sugary treats for her great grandkids, she did it for me, too! My favorite Pop-Tart was the simplest of them all, the cinnamon and brown sugar variety. I made this version to mimic the classic Mombo kept in her cupboard for me.

1 recipe Pie Dough (page 28)

Cinnamon Smear Filling
1 cup firmly packed dark brown sugar
1 tablespoon honey
1 large egg
½ teaspoon vanilla extract
¾ cup (1½ sticks) unsalted butter, melted
1 tablespoon all-purpose flour
1 tablespoon ground cinnamon

Brown Sugar Glaze
1 cup firmly packed dark brown sugar
¼ cup whole milk
¼ cup (½ stick) unsalted butter
Pinch of kosher salt
½ teaspoon vanilla extract

To make the cinnamon smear filling, whisk together the brown sugar, honey, egg, and vanilla. Add the butter and whisk until smooth. Stir in the flour and cinnamon.

The filling can be made ahead and stored in the fridge for up to 2 weeks. When ready to use, allow the smear to sit on the counter and come to room temperature before spreading it on the pie dough.

Preheat the oven to 350°F. Lightly grease a baking sheet with canola oil or line with parchment paper.

To make the pop tarts, roll out the pie dough into a ¼-inch-thick rectangle. Using a pizza cutter and a straight edge, cut the dough into even rectangles about 3 by 5 inches.

Spread 1 teaspoon of the filling in the center of a dough rectangle, leaving ¼ inch of empty space around the edges. Place another rectangle of dough on top to sandwich the filling in the middle. Use a fork to press a seam all the way around the edges and to pierce holes on the top of the tart to vent air during baking.

Place the tarts 1 inch apart on the prepared baking sheet. Bake for 15 to 20 minutes, until light golden brown.

continued

Immediately remove them from the baking sheet and place on a rack to cool completely.

To make the brown sugar glaze, heat all of the ingredients in a medium saucepan over medium heat and bring to a boil. Allow the mixture to bubble for 2 minutes, then transfer it to the bowl of a stand mixer fitted with a whisk attachment. Beat on medium speed until the bowl is cool to the touch, about 10 minutes. The mixture will have the consistency of honey. Tarts will keep wrapped airtight at room temperature for up to 3 days.

HAND PIES

These hand pies are the less fancy version of a Pop-Tart. They can be filled with fresh fruits, and toppings aren't required. These are a great way to use your farmer's market finds.

1 recipe Pie Dough (page 28)
½ cup fruit jam and/or fresh fruit, for filling

Preheat the oven to 350°F. Line a baking sheet with parchment paper.

Roll the pie dough into a ¼-inch-thick rectangle. Using a pizza cutter or knife, cut the dough into 3 by 3-inch squares or 4-inch circles.

Brush the edges of one square or circle with water. Place 1 teaspoon of the jam in the center, leaving ½ inch of dough around the edge. Or try ½ teaspoon of the jam topped with a few fresh berries or diced raw apples.

Place a second circle or square on top of the filling. Use a fork to press around the edges, sealing the pie together. Use the fork to pierce vent holes on top. Place on the prepared baking sheet, about 1 inch apart.

Bake for about 25 minutes, or until the pies start to brown. Immediately remove from the baking sheet and place on a rack to cool completely. Hand pies will keep wrapped airtight at room temperature for up to 3 days.

BREAD

Age 22, *the Culinary Institute of America:* I thought my chef-instructor was superhuman: he was able to rattle bread recipes off the top of his head. He could tell when the dough needed more water or more flour just by the sound it made in the mixer. Without even looking at the loaves or setting a timer, he knew when it was time to take them out of the oven. I wanted, more than anything, to know what he knew, so I could be just like him in the bakery of my dreams.

Yeast became my obsession.

Age 23, *Bread Alone, the baking institution in the Catskills:* My first paying job as a baker—only they weren't hiring bakers. I took a job as a barista just so I could get my foot in the door. My shift started at 7 a.m., so I showed up at 3 a.m. and wiggled my way into the bakery. I learned just enough Spanish to communicate with the team of bakers and ask permission to "help."

They gave me a space on the bread line and plopped a lump of dough in front of me. I watched them shape loaf after loaf on the conveyor belt. I tried to follow their lead and mimic their technique, but my dough quickly became too sticky to work with: it covered my hands. How did these bakers stay so clean? Why were their loaves so smooth? After weeks of practice, I could finally hold my own on the shaping line. Soon, I learned how to load the giant wood-fired oven with fluffy loaves of focaccia. Before I knew it, I was plucked out from behind the espresso maker and given a job on the baking team.

Age 25, *Amy's Bread, Manhattan:* My shift started at 9 p.m. and finished just before the sun came up over New York City. I lived in a horrible basement apartment in Queens. I did everything to avoid being at home. As soon as I woke up, I hopped on the E train from Roosevelt station and went straight to Chelsea. I wandered around town, getting my favorite French onion soup from Pastis and a cupcake from Magnolia Bakery. Eventually, I gave up on the wandering and went to work early, just like I'd done at Bread Alone. I spent hours watching Wayne mix organic dough and Patrick mix French dough for baguettes before the rest of the night crew arrived to start baking. Before long, I knew the ins and outs of every baking position. When one of the assistant night managers went on maternity leave, owner Amy Scherber promoted me. Just a few months later, I was given the title of production manager, a role I never expected to get this early in my career.

Age 30, *Tribeca Oven, northern New Jersey:* After marrying and struggling to make ends meet with one-year-old Josie and newborn Keegan, I took a corporate job handling recipe development for a company that shipped partially baked and flash-frozen artisan breads all over the country. I traveled all over the United States to meet with Target, Hyatt, the Cheesecake Factory, Wegmans, Whole Foods, Kroger, Big Y, Unos, and HMSHost, helping all of them to develop the perfect bread for their needs. I worked with a team to develop weight, height, and length specifications for each bread based on hours of testing. I enrolled in an MBA program to better understand how to market my new creations. It also helped me to conduct the financial analysis and profit potential of new products before they launched.

Making myself indispensable, working fifteen-hour days, and flying to two different cities a week . . . it wasn't enough to break the glass ceiling at Tribeca. When my boss told me "You're not really management material, with your three kids and all . . .," I knew it was time for me to move on.

Age 32, *Montclair Bread Co., Montclair, New Jersey:* I unlocked the door for the first time at 2 a.m. in May 2012. The previous owners had retired and moved, and it was my best chance to carve out my own path. I was taking a huge risk: the modest amount of capital I'd raised through investments from friends largely went to pay for equipment and inventory. My husband, three children, and I were on food stamps and Medicaid, and we faced foreclosure on our home. I had less than $2,500 in my opening bank account and no choice but to make it work.

That morning, I opened the oven to remove a batch of bread and the door fell off in my hand. The whole thing crashed to the floor. I noticed the hole in the bathroom floor was so large you could see into the basement. I realized that the electricity was unstable. Then, the first customer to walk through the door burst into tears as soon as she saw me and my breads behind the counter. She had expected to see the previous owners and their vegan and gluten-free offerings.

I invited my friends to come by for coffee and croissants on the house. I asked them to sit outside to enjoy them so people walking by would notice.

CURRANT SEEDED BREAD

When I was pregnant with my daughter, Josie, I gained eighty-five pounds. It was quite a shock for someone who previously was the annoying girl who could eat an entire chocolate cake and lose ten pounds. My midwife told me I needed to stop eating bread. I had a better idea. I decided to develop a bread recipe that would include all the vitamins and nutrients she told me I needed to eat. I included blackstrap molasses for iron, flax for omega-3s, pumpkin seeds for B vitamins and potassium, and currants for vitamin C, magnesium, and more B vitamins. The loaves were made with 100 percent whole-grain flours. I even had the recipe certified by the Cleveland Clinic with their seal of approval for healthy foods, and the bread later won the America's Best Raisin Bread competition.

Levain (starter)
- 1 cup whole wheat flour
- 1/3 cup cool tap water
- 1/4 cup Mature Sourdough Starter, 8 to 12 hours after the last feeding (page xxii)
- 1 tablespoon rye flour

Bread
- 1 cup cool tap water
- 2 cups whole wheat flour
- 1 teaspoon blackstrap molasses
- 1/4 teaspoon instant yeast
- 1 1/2 teaspoons kosher salt
- 1 1/2 cups dried Zante currants or raisins
- 1/3 cup sunflower seeds
- 1/3 cup pumpkin seeds
- 1 tablespoon hemp seeds
- 1 tablespoon sesame seeds
- 1 1/2 tablespoons whole flaxseeds

4 or 5 ice cubes

To make the levain, mix together the whole wheat flour, water, sourdough starter, and rye flour in a glass or plastic container with a lid. It should be big enough to allow the levain to expand to twice its size. Let it sit at room temperature for 8 to 12 hours before you plan to make the final dough.

continued

To make the bread, combine the levain, water, flour, molasses, and yeast together in the bowl of a stand mixer fitted with a dough hook, or follow the "Hand-Mixing Bread Dough" instructions (see page xviii). Mix on low speed for 3 to 4 minutes. The ingredients will come together to form a ball. Add the salt and mix on medium-high speed for another 6 minutes, or until the ball of dough starts to curl around the dough hook. Add the currants and all the seeds. Mix on low for 1 to 2 minutes, until the fruit and seeds are evenly incorporated.

Place the dough into an airtight container. Let it rest for 30 minutes at room temperature.

Grease two 8-inch cake pans, two 8½ by 4½-inch loaf pans, or two baking sheets with canola oil. Divide the dough into two equal pieces. Shape each piece into an 8-inch log (for loaves) or fold into a round (for cake pans) and place into the prepared pans. You can also shape freeform loaves on the baking sheets. Cover the loaves with plastic wrap or an unscented kitchen-sized garbage bag and let them rise for 2 to 3 hours at room temperature, until they crest out of the loaf pans.

Preheat the oven to 375°F. Set one oven rack at the lowest setting, then place an empty baking sheet on the rack. After you place the bread dough in the oven and before closing the oven door, throw the ice cubes on the baking sheet. Quickly shut the door to allow the resulting steam to be trapped inside. This will moisten the surface of the loaves and give them a nice big spring!

Bake for 20 to 30 minutes, until the loaves are deep brown in color and sound hollow when tapped. Remove them from their pans and let them cool completely before slicing. The interior of this bread is very moist and can be gummy if it is sliced when warm. Loaves will keep wrapped lightly in a tea towel at room temperature for up to 3 days,or they can be wrapped airtight and frozen for several months.

BAGUETTES

Makes 2 baguettes

"You need more esteem," Miguel shouted at me from across the bakery. "Your baguettes will look better if you have more esteem!"

I couldn't believe it. My five-foot-tall coworker usually spent the overnight shift at Amy's Bread telling me I was a terrible baker: "My grandmother is faster than you, and she's in a wheelchair and she has only one arm," he once yelled at me. Now he was telling me that if I just had a little more confidence in myself, my baguettes would be more beautiful.

"Thank you, Miguel, that means a lot to me. I'll get it right one day soon," I responded.

"No, you idiot, not esteem, eh-STEAM. Your bread needs STEAM!!!! Hold the button longer!!!" he raged. Oh, right, steam. The steam in the oven allows the baguettes to rise more and gives them a thin, crispy crust and bright sheen. He didn't care about my self-confidence, just the right amount of eh-steam. But he was right: from then on, my baguettes came out perfectly.

Every single time I pull a perfect baguette out of the oven, I feel validated. Flour, water, yeast, and salt mixed in just the right way, deep brown crust pulling up and away from the center of the loaf with crisp, slightly charred edges. There is truly nothing that makes me happier than a baguette that tells me I did everything right.

This recipe uses a *poolish*—a traditional French starter composed of equal amounts of flour and water with a pinch of yeast. The *poolish* is made eight to twelve hours before the final dough. It enhances the flavor, acts as a natural preservative, and creates more fermentation in the final dough, which gives the baguettes their light texture.

Poolish (starter)
¼ cup cool tap water
½ cup all-purpose flour
⅛ teaspoon instant dry yeast

Bread
1 cup cool tap water
2 cups all-purpose flour
½ teaspoon instant dry yeast
1 teaspoon kosher salt

4 or 5 ice cubes

To make the *poolish*, mix the water, flour, and yeast together in a glass or plastic container with a lid that will allow the *poolish* to expand to twice its volume. Let it sit at room temperature for 8 to 12 hours. When it is ready to use, it will have big air bubbles under the surface.

To make the bread dough, combine the cool water, flour, yeast, and salt together in a large plastic container (16 by 11 by 4 inches works well) with a lid. Use your hands to combine the mixture. You do not need to knead the dough; just combine all the ingredients so there are no dry spots and everything is incorporated. It will look ROUGH, and that's okay. As you move through the resting/ folding process, it will begin to resemble a real dough. Please refrain from any urges to start kneading it with all your might, unless you just want to burn a few extra calories today.

Place the lid on the container and let the dough rest for 30 minutes at room temperature.

After the rest, stretch and fold all four sides of the dough into the center, allowing them to overlap, as if you were wrapping a present (see page xviii). Flip the dough over so the sides do not unravel.

Cover and let the dough rest for another 30 minutes.

Repeat the folding process once more. Let the dough rest for 30 minutes more.

continued

Turn the dough out on a floured work surface. Divide the dough into four equal pieces. Roll each piece into a fat 2 by 4-inch log. Cover the dough with plastic wrap or an unscented kitchen-sized garbage bag so it doesn't dry out. Let the dough relax for 15 minutes. This will make each piece easier to roll into a long baguette.

Once the dough has relaxed, working with one piece at a time, tighten the log by pressing the furthest edge of the dough to the center of the dough. Repeat this step once more, then fold the furthest edge of the dough all the way to meet the bottom edge. Using the palm of your hand, press firmly on the edge of the dough to seal it and create a seam. Repeat with the remaining dough logs.

Think back to the last time you made a snake out of clay and roll each log out into a long, skinny baguette. The goal is to reach 18 inches, but if the surface of the dough starts to tear, break, and turn into a sticky mess—stop where you are. A 15-inch baguette will taste the same as an 18-inch baguette.

Line a 13 by 18-inch baking sheet with parchment paper. Place two baguettes on the sheet, 4 inches apart. Cover with plastic wrap or an unscented kitchen-sized garbage bag and let rise for 20 minutes.

While you are waiting for your baguettes to rise, preheat the oven to 450°F. Set one oven rack at the lowest setting, then place an empty baking sheet on the rack.

Uncover the dough. Using a serrated knife, slash the surface of the baguettes. You can cut one straight line or try cutting the traditional five short lines. The blade should be at a 45-degree angle when cutting in order to have the dough's "ears" (as bakers call the cuts) open up and stand at attention.

Put the baguettes in the oven. Before closing the oven door, throw the ice cubes on the baking sheet in the bottom of the oven. Quickly shut the door to allow the resulting steam to be trapped inside. This will moisten the surface of the loaves.

Bake for approximately 20 minutes, or until the baguettes have reached a deep golden brown similar to a caramel candy.

Try to avoid consuming all of your baguettes immediately after pulling them from the oven. One, you will burn yourself and regret it later, and, two, hot bread just tastes like hot bread. To truly appreciate the fruits of your labor and to taste all the subtleties of flavor you've created, eat it at room temperature. Baguettes will keep wrapped lightly in a tea towel at room temperature for 24 to 48 hours maximum. They are best eaten fresh. (Wrapping them in plastic wrap will soften the crust.) They can be wrapped airtight and frozen for several months. Popping them back in the oven at 350°F for 8 minutes will refresh them.

CHALLAH

I spent six months in 2004 working in Rochester, New York, at the flagship bakery for Wegmans, a large Northeast grocery chain. I helped develop recipes for breads that would be rolled out to all of their stores. I braided hundreds of loaves of challah each week. With help and encouragement from my fellow bakers, Justin and Doug, braiding became my special skill.

When I started baking challah at Montclair Bread Company, I taught my then-four-year-old daughter, Josie, how to braid along with me. She picked it up fast. She still wakes up early every Friday morning to help the bakers braid challah each week. She has trained many an adult baker to braid along with her.

¼ cup vegetable oil

6 large egg yolks

1 tablespoon honey

1 cup cool tap water

3 cups all-purpose flour

2 teaspoons instant dry yeast

1½ teaspoons kosher salt

1 large egg, beaten, for brushing the challah before it bakes

Place the oil, egg yolks, honey, and water in the bowl of a stand mixer fitted with a dough hook. Add the flour, yeast, and salt. Mix the ingredients on medium speed for 10 to 12 minutes, until a tight ball forms and you can stretch a small piece of dough so thin you can see through it.

Divide the dough into two equal pieces. Divide each piece into three or six equal portions, depending on how many strands you want to braid. Gently shape each strand into a little log. Cover the logs and let them rest at room temperature for 30 minutes.

Work the logs into longer ropes about 12 inches long. This process should be like making snakes out of clay. Pinch the strands together at one end and create a dough braid, pinching the strands together when the braid is finished and tucking them under to seal. Avoid the two biggest braiding mistakes: rolling the strands too long and skinny and braiding too tight, which doesn't allow for the bread to rise. Keep the braid chubby and loose! Repeat with the remaining dough.

Place both loaves on a standard baking sheet, about 6 inches apart. Cover them loosely with plastic wrap or an unscented kitchen-sized garbage bag and let them rise at room temperature for 2 hours. You'll know they're ready when you can poke the dough with your finger and still be able to see an indent 30 seconds later.

Preheat the oven to 375°F.

Brush the beaten egg over the surface of the dough (get in all the nooks and crannies).

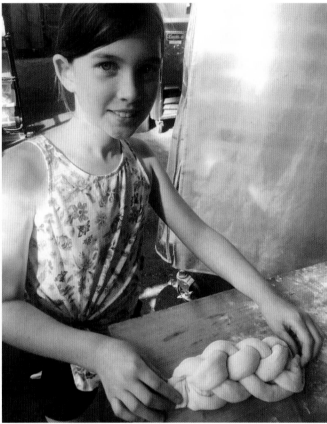

Bake for 20 to 25 minutes, until deep mahogany brown. The creases in the braid should still be light in color but starting to brown. Remove the loaves from the pan and let cool on a wire rack or a wooden cutting board, which will absorb the heat and prevent condensation. Loaves will keep wrapped airtight at room temperature for up to 3 days. In order to keep them soft, they can be placed in a resealable plastic bag or wrapped in plastic wrap.

Rosemary Sourdough Bread

SOURDOUGH BREAD

Makes 2 loaves

When I started at the Culinary Institute of America, I knew nothing about yeast and even less about the wild yeast cultivated in a sourdough starter. On day 1 of Hearth Breads and Rolls, Chef Nick Greco taught us about the different strains of yeast and the twelve steps of breadmaking with such passion it was impossible not to beg for more. I stayed through every lunch break and every dinner break. I volunteered to help with adult baking classes on the weekends. One weekend, Chef Greco asked me to take the sourdough starter home. I had to feed it and keep it alive until 3 a.m. Monday, when we would need to use it to make bread rise in class. I followed his instructions exactly: Add equal parts flour, water, and starter at 3 p.m. Sunday. Make sure the water is exactly 70°F.

After feeding the starter, I positioned the tall, round tub in front of my apartment door. That way I wouldn't forget to take it with me in my 2:30 a.m. sleepiness. That morning, when my alarm woke me from a dead sleep, I grabbed my bag and turned to head out the door. What I saw stopped me in my tracks. The sourdough had bubbled up out of its home and invaded mine. The yeasty beige sludge bubbled and lurked across the entire entryway, making its way deep into the carpet. Now it wasn't just about getting the sourdough to class in time to make the bread. I didn't know how I was going to escape from my apartment!

I hastily closed the lid of the sourdough tub and scooped as much of the goo as possible into the garbage before running out the door. When I arrived, I told Chef Greco what happened. He asked, "What temperature is your apartment?" It was a hot summer in Poughkeepsie, and I didn't have air-conditioning. When he relayed the instructions, he didn't account for my 90° living space. The wild yeast grew out of control, and there was nothing I could have done to stop it. I keep in touch with my landlord, who said he was still picking sourdough remnants out of the carpet years after the incident.

4 cups all-purpose flour

¼ cup whole wheat flour

1½ cups Mature Sourdough Starter, 8 to 12 hours after the last feeding (page xxii)

1½ teaspoon kosher salt

2 cups cool tap water

4 or 5 ice cubes

continued

In a large mixing bowl, mix together the flours, starter, and salt. Add the water and work the dough into a compact ball. No need to knead; just gather all the ingredients until they are incorporated.

Cover with plastic wrap or an unscented kitchen-sized garbage bag and let the dough rest for 1 hour.

Stretch and fold all four sides of the dough into the center, allowing them to overlap as if you were wrapping a present (see page xviii). Flip the dough over so the sides do not unravel. Cover and let it rest for another hour.

Turn the dough out on a floured work surface. Divide the dough into two equal pieces. Pat one piece into a 4 by 6-inch rectangle. Pick up one of the shorter ends and fold the dough to the middle of the rectangle. Press in with your fingertips, working with as little flour as possible. (The flour prevents the dough from sealing, which will create a giant hole in the center of the loaf. You are creating tension along the surface, which will help to trap gas inside as the loaf expands. This is how you get an open airy "crumb" inside the loaf.) Fold the dough again, so it meets the other short end, and use the heel of your hand to press down, sealing it all up. Give your loaf a little wiggle to even it out.

Sprinkle flour onto a standard baking sheet. Place the loaf seam side down onto the floured sheet.

Repeat the process with the other piece of dough and place it on the baking sheet, leaving 4 inches between the loaves. Cover with plastic wrap or an unscented kitchen-sized garbage bag (fold the bag so that it's airtight) and let the loaves rise at room temperature for 1 hour. Then refrigerate for the next 8 to 12 hours.

After the loaves have enjoyed their cold ferment, remove from the fridge. Leave them covered and allow the dough to come to room temperature, about 1 to 2 hours.

Preheat the oven to 450°F. Set one oven rack at the lowest setting, then place an empty baking sheet on the rack. Once the dough is at room temperature, use a sharp knife to carefully cut a ¼-inch-deep slash down the center of each loaf, end to end.

After you place the bread in the oven and before closing the oven door, throw the ice cubes on the baking sheet in the bottom of the oven. Quickly shut the door to allow the resulting steam to be trapped inside. This will moisten the surface of the loaves.

Bake for 25 to 28 minutes, until the loaves have turned a deep brown. Remove from the tray and allow to cool on a cutting board or cooling rack completely before eating. Sourdough loaves will keep wrapped lightly in a tea towel at room temperature for up to 5 days! Wrapping them in plastic wrap will soften the crust. I keep my loaves cut side down on my cutting board (they never last for 5 days in my house). They can be wrapped airtight and frozen for several months. Popping them back in the oven at 350°F for 8 minutes will refresh them.

Variations:

ROSEMARY SOURDOUGH

Add the leaves from two sprigs of fresh rosemary into the water before mixing the dough—no need to chop them. NOTE: It's important to use fresh rosemary and not dried. It is easier to eat. Sometimes dried rosemary is worse than a splinter of wood when you bite into it! The fresh-picked leaves also have oils in them that release into the dough during the mixing process. This ensures that the whole loaf will taste like rosemary, even when you're not biting into an actual piece of the herb.

WHOLE WHEAT SOURDOUGH

Use whole wheat flour for the last feeding of the starter. Replace 1 cup of white flour in the final dough with whole wheat flour.

GUINNESS MICHE

Use rye flour for the last feeding of the starter. Replace 1½ cups of white flour in the final dough with whole wheat flour. Replace the water with Guinness stout.

STOLLEN

Before attending the Culinary Institute of America, I had never heard of stollen, a traditional holiday bread from Dresden, Germany, that is meant to represent a swaddled baby Jesus. The first time I got to taste it was also the first time I made it myself with Chef Dieter Schorner's recipe. Chef Schorner, one of my professors at the Culinary Institute of America, was kind of like God and Grandpa all wrapped into one tiny German pastry chef. His wacky red hair and big blue eyes reminded me a bit of Professor Emmett "Doc" Brown from *Back to the Future*. He was credited with bringing crème brûlée to America and told stories about his catastrophic soufflé failure that left the Queen of England waiting for her dessert.

I pay tribute to the late Chef Schorner by making his stollen recipe each year to celebrate the holidays at Montclair Bread. The bakery team sets aside an entire day just after Thanksgiving to make hundreds of loaves of stollen to last through the season. We invite our customers to come watch and sample the loaves hot out of the oven.

Filling
4 ounces almond paste

¼ cup sugar

1 large egg white

½ cup sliced almonds

Sponge
1⅓ cups all-purpose flour

½ teaspoon kosher salt

1½ teaspoons instant yeast

½ cup whole milk, at room temperature

Dough
½ cup diced candied lemon and/or orange peel

1 cup dried currants or raisins

2 tablespoons (1 ounce) almond paste

¼ cup sugar

¾ cup (1½ sticks) unsalted butter, at room temperature

1 teaspoon vanilla extract

1⅓ cups all-purpose flour

½ teaspoon kosher salt

½ cup sliced almonds

Topping
½ cup (1 stick) unsalted butter, melted

1 cup confectioners' sugar

To make the filling (up to one week ahead), place the almond paste and sugar in the bowl of a stand mixer fitted with a paddle attachment. Mix on medium speed until the almond paste breaks down into small pebbles. Add the egg white and continue mixing until the batter is smooth. Add the sliced almonds on low speed until they are evenly distributed throughout the filling. Divide into two lumps and shape into 6-inch-long logs. Wrap the logs tightly in plastic wrap and store them at room temperature.

To make the sponge, combine the flour, salt, yeast, and milk in the bowl of a stand mixer fitted with a dough hook. Mix on low speed for 3 minutes, or until the ingredients combine to form a ball of dough.

Spray cooking spray or brush oil along the inside of a large bowl. Place the sponge dough in the oiled bowl and cover with plastic wrap or an unscented kitchen-sized garbage bag. Let it rise at room temperature (68° to 72°F) for 1 hour.

To make the dough, combine the candied fruit and currants in a strainer. Rinse them under cold water to remove excess sugars from the outside of the dried fruits. Set aside and allow any excess water to drain off while you are assembling the rest of the dough.

Place the almond paste and sugar in the bowl of a stand mixer fitted with a paddle attachment. Mix on medium speed until the almond paste breaks down into small pebbles. Add the butter and vanilla and cream the ingredients until the mixture is fluffy and light in color.

Remove the paddle attachment and fit the stand mixer with a dough hook.

Add the risen sponge, flour, and salt to the bowl with the creamed mixture. Mix on medium speed for 8 minutes, or until the dough forms a tight ball and starts to wind itself up the dough hook.

Add the almonds and rinsed fruit. Mix the dough on low speed for an additional 3 to 4 minutes, until the fruit and almonds are evenly distributed throughout the dough. Cover the top of the bowl with plastic wrap or an unscented kitchen-sized garbage bag and let it rest at room temperature for 30 minutes.

Turn the dough out on a floured work surface. Divide the dough into two equal pieces. Shape one piece into a 5 by 7-inch rectangle. Turn the rectangle lengthwise and use the pinky side of your hand to press a trench into the center of the dough. Press an almond log into the trench. Fold one side of the dough over the log and press into the other side to seal. Repeat with the other piece of dough.

continued

Line a standard baking sheet with parchment paper. Place both loaves seam side down, onto the sheet, at least 6 inches apart. Cover the loaves with plastic wrap or an unscented kitchen-sized garbage bag and let rest for 2 hours. They are very dense and will barely increase in size before they are ready to bake.

Preheat the oven to 350°F. Bake the loaves for 45 minutes, or until the crust is a deep brown. Pick off and discard any burned fruit. Let the loaves cool slightly on the baking sheet while making the topping.

To make the topping, gather two small roasting pans or baking sheets that are roughly the size of a loaf. Pour the butter into one pan and the sugar into another. While the loaves are still warm, carefully roll each loaf in the butter, coating the entire exterior; then place the buttery loaf into the sugar and roll it around until it is completely coated in sugar. Repeat with the second loaf.

Allow the loaves to cool completely on a rack before tightly sealing them in plastic wrap. Loaves will keep wrapped airtight at room temperature for up to 3 months. The butter and sugar crust acts as a preservative.

CIABATTA

Bread lore says there was a baker in Italy who was supposed to make baguettes for the restaurant where he worked. He added too much water to the dough, and the resulting loaves were flat, dusty, and full of wide-open holes. They resembled bedroom slippers, or *ciabatta* in Italian. The next night, the restaurant patrons begged for more ciabatta, and so it was.

2 cups all-purpose flour

¼ cup durum flour

1 cup cool tap water

½ cup Mature Sourdough Starter, 8 to 12 hours after the last feeding (page xxii)

¼ teaspoon instant yeast

1 teaspoon kosher salt

4 or 5 ice cubes

In a large mixing bowl, combine all of the ingredients together until a shaggy dough ball forms. Let the dough rest for 45 minutes in a glass or plastic container with a lid. After the rest, stretch and fold all four sides of the dough into the center, allowing them to overlap, as if you were wrapping a present (see page xviii). Flip the dough over so the sides do not unravel. Replace the lid and let the dough rest for another 45 minutes.

Stretch and fold the four dough sides a second time, return to the container, replace the lid, and let the dough rest for a final 45 minutes.

Turn the dough out on a heavily floured work surface. Gently press the dough into a 4 by 11-inch rectangle. Use a pizza cutter or a bench knife to cut the dough into two equally sized loaves. If you want to make sandwich rolls, cut each loaf into thirds so the dough chunks resemble squares.

Flour a baking sheet. Place the loaves or rolls onto the sheet, 4 inches apart. Cover with plastic wrap or an unscented kitchen-sized garbage bag (fold the ends under to keep the bag airtight). Let them rise for 2 hours.

Preheat the oven to 450°F. Set one oven rack at the lowest setting, then place an empty baking sheet on the rack.

continued

Flip the loaves over onto a clean baking sheet so the bottom becomes the top. If you don't have a steam setting on the oven, after you place the bread dough in the oven and before closing the oven door, throw the ice cubes on the baking sheet on the bottom rack of the oven. Quickly shut the door to allow the resulting steam to be trapped inside. This will moisten the surface of your loaves. Bake for 20 to 25 minutes, until the loaves are a deep brown and start to crack at the edges. Ciabatta will keep wrapped lightly in a tea towel at room temperature for 24 to 48 hours maximum. They are best eaten fresh. (Wrapping them in plastic wrap will soften the crust.) They can be wrapped airtight and frozen for several months. Popping them back in the oven at 350°F for 8 minutes will refresh them.

OLIVE CIABATTA

This is far and away the Montclair Bread Company staff favorite. This bread with a bowl of balsamic vinegar, some extra-virgin olive oil, and a few slices of prosciutto is all I need for a summer dinner. Add ½ cup pitted kalamata olives, 1 tablespoon fresh thyme leaves, and 1 tablespoon extra-virgin olive oil with the rest of the ingredients. Proceed with the recipe as directed.

PRETZELS

Makes 8 pretzels

Every summer, I host a summer baking camp at Montclair Bread Co. Five days, two dozen tiny bakers, and all the carbs you can eat. Spaces fill up before spring, and campers come back year after year to bake with our team.

Our campers love making pretzels almost as much as they love eating them. Pretzels were created by Catholic monks in the Middle Ages to be given as a reward to children who said their prayers. Back then, instead of putting their hands together to pray, parishioners crossed their arms and placed their hands on opposite shoulders to pray—just like the twist of the pretzel.

Pretzels were once used in wedding ceremonies, too. Couples twisted the dough together to "tie the knot" and become one. Such a rich history for a little lump of bread.

2½ cups all-purpose flour

2 teaspoons instant yeast

1½ teaspoons kosher salt

1 tablespoon unsalted butter, at room temperature

1 cup cold tap water

½ teaspoon molasses, maple syrup, honey, dark beer, or dark corn syrup

2 tablespoons baking soda

6 cups water

Coarse salt, for sprinkling

In the bowl of a stand mixer fitted with a dough hook, mix the flour, yeast, salt, butter, water, and molasses on low speed until the ingredients are incorporated. The dough will look dry and stiff. Turn the mixer to medium-high speed and mix for 10 minutes, until it is tightly wound around the hook and the surface is smooth.

Leave the dough in the mixing bowl, cover with plastic wrap, and let rest for 30 minutes. Divide the dough into eight equal lumps and roll each lump into a little log. Cover the logs and let rest for another 30 minutes before rolling each into a skinny strand about 12 inches long, like making snakes out of clay.

To shape the pretzels, make a big, exaggerated loop at the top and cross it at the bottom. Twist a second time at the bottom. Press the bottom ends into the top of the loop. Flip the pretzel over and wiggle the knot so that the openings are even.

continued

Place the pretzels on a baking sheet. Cover them with plastic wrap or an unscented kitchen-sized garbage bag and refrigerate them for 2 hours.

Preheat the oven to 350°F. Spray a baking sheet with cooking spray.

Heat the baking soda with the water in a wide pot over medium-high heat. Bring the water to a boil, then decrease to low heat and simmer. Remove the pretzels from the fridge. Dip each pretzel into the water and let it cook for 5 seconds before using a slotted spoon to gently remove it. Place the pretzel on the baking sheet. Make sure the little nubs/ends of the pretzel strands are down on the sheet so they don't pop open when baked. Sprinkle with salt. Repeat this process until all the pretzels are dipped and salted. Place them on a standard baking sheet, 2 inches apart.

Bake the pretzels for 10 to 15 minutes, until they have a deep golden brown crust. Pretzels will keep wrapped airtight at room temperature for up to 2 days, though they are best eaten on the day they are made.

JALAPENO-CHEDDAR CORN BREAD

Makes 2 loaves

I've been working on this recipe since I was a student at the Culinary Institute of America. It is based on a traditional Portuguese *broa*, a yeasted corn bread. Creating the porridge first softens the cornmeal, which creates an airier loaf.

My friend Peter hosted a chili cook-off one year. I added jalapeno and cheddar to my corn bread so that it would pair perfectly with my chili recipe. Peter loved it so much he asked me to make 200 rolls for a chili dinner he hosted later. Now this bread appears on the Montclair Bread Company menu every January for football playoff/chili season and every August when fresh Jersey corn is being harvested.

Corn Porridge

¼ cup coarse yellow corn meal

½ cup boiling tap water

Corn Biga

1 cup all-purpose flour

½ cup cold water

¼ teaspoon instant yeast

Dough

3 cups all-purpose flour

⅓ cup water

1½ teaspoons instant yeast

1 teaspoon kosher salt

1 small jalapeno, deveined, seeded, and diced

Corn kernels cut from 1 ear corn, or ½ cup defrosted frozen corn

1 cup small-diced sharp cheddar cheese, or ½ cup grated sharp cheddar cheese

4 or 5 ice cubes

Prepare the porridge and the biga 12 to 24 hours before you mix the final dough.

To make the porridge, place the cornmeal in a small glass or plastic container with a lid. Pour the boiling water over the cornmeal and stir to hydrate all of the grains. Cover with the lid and let sit at room temperature for at least 12 hours.

To make the biga, mix the flour, water, and yeast by hand in a mixing bowl (or in the bowl of a stand mixer fitted with a dough hook) until all the ingredients are combined into a stiff ball of dough, about 1 minute. Place the biga in a glass or plastic container with a lid. Make sure it has enough space to double in size. Cover and let sit at room temperature for at least 12 hours. continued

To make the dough, combine the porridge, biga, flour, water, yeast, and salt in the bowl of a stand mixer fitted with a dough hook, or follow the "Hand-Mixing Bread Dough" instructions (see page xviii). If using a mixer, mix on low speed for about 2 minutes, or until all the ingredients come together to form a ball. Increase to medium speed for about 6 minutes, or until the dough starts to climb up the hook. Return the mixer to low speed, add the corn, jalapenos, and cheese, and mix for 3 minutes more, until everything is evenly distributed throughout the dough. Remove the dough from the bowl and fold in any bits and pieces of veggies that remain at the bottom of the mixing bowl. Place the dough in another bowl, greased with canola oil, and cover with plastic wrap, or place the dough in an airtight container. Let rise for 1 hour.

Turn the dough out on a floured work surface. Divide the dough into two equal pieces. Pat one piece into a 4 by 6-inch rectangle. Pick up one of the shorter ends and fold the dough to the middle of the rectangle. Press in with your fingertips, working with as little flour as possible, so that the dough adheres to itself. (You are creating tension along the surface, which will help to trap gas inside as the loaf expands. This is how you get an open, airy "crumb" inside the loaf.) Fold the dough again, so it meets the other short end, and use the heel of your hand to press down, sealing it all up. Give your loaf a little wiggle to even it out.

Sprinkle flour onto a standard baking sheet. Place the loaf, seam side down, onto the sheet. Repeat the folding process with the other piece of dough and place that on the sheet, keeping the loaves at least 4 inches apart. Cover with plastic wrap or an unscented kitchen-sized garbage bag (fold the bag around the edge of the pan so that it's airtight), and let the loaves rise at room temperature for 2 hours.

Preheat the oven to 450°F. Set one oven rack at the lowest setting, then place an empty baking sheet on the rack. Use a sharp knife to carefully cut a ¼-inch-deep slash down the center of each loaf, end to end.

After you place the bread in the oven and before closing the oven door, throw the ice cubes on the baking sheet on the bottom rack of the oven. Quickly shut the door to allow the resulting steam to be trapped inside. This will moisten the surface of the loaves. Bake for 25 to 28 minutes, until the loaves have turned a deep brown. Remove them from the baking sheet and allow the loaves to cool completely before eating. These loaves will keep at room temperature for up to 3 days. Wrap them in plastic wrap for softer bread or in a tea towel for crispier loaves.

Variations

OATMEAL-APRICOT PORRIDGE BREAD

In the porridge, use steel-cut oats instead of cornmeal; in the *biga*, swap whole wheat flour for all-purpose flour. In the final dough, increase the water to ½ cup, decrease the yeast to 1 teaspoon, increase the salt to 1½ teaspoons, add 1 cup finely diced dried apricots, and omit the jalapeno, corn, and cheddar cheese.

MULTIGRAIN PORRIDGE BREAD

In the porridge, use a grain mix, such as Bob's Red Mill 10 Grain Hot Cereal, instead of the cornmeal; in the *biga*, swap whole wheat flour for all-purpose flour. In the final dough, increase the water to ½ cup, decrease the yeast to 1 teaspoon, increase the salt to 1½ teaspoons, add ½ cup sunflower seeds and ½ cup flaxseeds, and omit the jalapeno, corn, and cheddar cheese.

Use It in a Sandwich

The bakery is located a half a block away from a train station that provides direct access to midtown Manhattan. I wanted to create premade sandwiches that commuters could grab as they headed for the train. The sandwiches are also a way to showcase a few of my breads.

SPICY ITALIAN

Makes 1 sandwich

For as long as I can remember, this has been my go-to sandwich at any deli. In Maryland, I grew up adding a spicy pepper relish to my subs. I didn't know it was a regional spread until I left the state and couldn't find it anywhere. When I added the Italian Sandwich to the menu at Montclair Bread Company, the first thing I did was lock down a spicy pepper relish supplier.

Slice one ciabatta roll (page 55) in half. Drizzle 1 teaspoon balsamic vinegar and 1 teaspoon olive oil on the top half of the roll. Spread 1 tablespoon spicy pepper relish on the bottom half of the roll. Layer two slices provolone cheese, two slices ham, two slices salami, and two slices capicola on the bottom roll. Top with two leaves of green lettuce and a thick slice of tomato before you close it up.

PEAR AND BRIE

Makes 3 sandwiches

This is the bakery's most popular sandwich. Cut one 18-inch baguette (page 42) in half. Whisk together one finely diced shallot, 1 tablespoon sliced capers, 1 tablespoon grainy mustard, 1 tablespoon lemon juice, and ½ cup red wine vinegar. While stirring or whisking the mixture, add 1⅓ cups olive oil slowly until it is completely incorporated. Add salt and pepper to taste.

Liberally drizzle the vinaigrette on both the top and bottom halves of the baguette. You will have extra vinaigrette. It will keep in the refrigerator for up to 4 weeks.

Layer two cored, thinly sliced Bartlett pears and 8 ounces sliced Brie on the bottom half of the baguette. Pile 5 ounces arugula on top of the pears. Close up the sandwich and cut it into thirds. You are picnic-ready.

HAM AND BRIE ON BUTTERED BAGUETTE
WITH CORNICHONS AND HARD-BOILED EGGS

Makes 3 sandwiches

When I lived in France, my French mom made these sandwiches for us to take to school for lunch. The combination is unlike anything I had eaten before. All the ingredients work together to provide a light, fresh sandwich. The butter keeps the baguette from getting soggy, making it great to take for picnics.

Slice the baguette (page 42) in half lengthwise. Spread 1 tablespoon salted butter on each side of the bread. Place five or six slices of boiled deli ham (or classic French Mandrange if you can find it) on the base of the bread. Slice 8 ounces Brie into long, thin pieces and layer them on top of the baguette. Slice three hard boiled eggs and position them on top of the cheese. Finally, cut 8 to 10 cornichons in half lengthwise and place them on top of the eggs. To add a little more crunch, top with the leaves of one head of endive before closing the sandwich. Cut into thirds.

CAPRESE

Makes 1 sandwich

Simple, classic, never disappoints, unless the tomato is tasteless and mealy. When I moved to Montclair, I didn't realize how seriously New Jersey takes tomatoes. I offer this sandwich only when tomato season is at its peak.

Slice one ciabatta roll (page 55) in half. Drizzle ½ teaspoon balsamic vinegar and ½ teaspoon olive oil on each half of the bread. Layer two ¼-inch-thick slices of tomato and one ¼-inch-thick slice of fresh mozzarella and top with four to six leaves of fresh basil.

GRILLED CHEESE ON ROSEMARY SOURDOUGH

Makes 1 sandwich

When I want a grilled cheese sandwich, I wait for the weekend when the Rosemary Sourdough is on the Montclair Bread Co. menu. Once you've made this grilled cheese, nothing else will do.

Cut two ½-inch-thick slices of Rosemary Sourdough (page 51). For larger sandwiches, don't be afraid to slice the loaf lengthwise instead of the traditional way. Spread a thin layer of mayonnaise on one side of each slice. Place three or four slices of sharp white cheddar cheese (or swap your favorite cheese) on the dry side of one slice of bread and top it with the other slice of bread, mayonnaise sides on the outside. Use a griddle or a sauté pan over medium heat to brown both sides of the sandwich and melt the cheese in the middle. Serve with your favorite tomato soup for dipping!

DOUGHNUTS

"While her bakery sells some of the best bread in the area, from ciabatta to a yeasted Cheddar cheese and jalapeño cornbread, it is the doughnuts for which people stand in line. Brioche makes for a less-sweet doughnut, which leaves [Rachel] and her team of bakers more room to experiment with toppings and fillings, a challenge it appears they have accepted with unabashed fervor."

—*New York Times*

"The red-and-green sprinkle-topped chocolate doughnut, on a brioche, is simply sensational."

—NJ.com

"The secret ingredient at Montclair Bread Company? It's her."

—The Backgrounder Podcast

From the outside, it was all sprinkles and ganache and long, long lines of hungry customers. I sat on the patio and read stories about doughnuts to children. I gave away prize boxes filled with treats, glazed, jelly, and tres leches topped with cherries. I organized a community street fair.

None of my customers guessed that beneath the surface, my personal life was imploding. The more public attention I got, the more appreciation I received, the more my husband sank into a jealous despair. He began to verbally abuse me in front of our children on a regular basis. I got so used to him calling me a "cunt" and a "bitch" that it started to feel normal. At times, he launched whatever object was closest at my head.

I began to spend more and more hours at the bakery, and not just because its success meant we could finally pay the rent and reliably buy groceries. It was now the only place I could avoid his wrath and the constant fighting.

It all came to a head the night I appeared on the Food Network's *Donut Showdown*. I had taped it eight months before and couldn't tell anyone that I had won. I couldn't wait for my hard work to be recognized on national TV and to finally be able to celebrate with my friends and family.

But from the beginning of the viewing party, it was clear something was wrong with Kevin. He headed to the bar immediately. While I was standing on a stool to thank all my friends, family, and customers for attending the party, he was slumped over on the bar shooting me a look of disgust. Would it have been so hard for him to publicly approve of my big win? To be the supportive husband I yearned for? A friend had to encourage him to stumble out of the party on home, where he picked a fight with my father before falling asleep.

What should have been one of the best nights of my life ended in disappointment and anxiety. How could I maintain a professional reputation in the community with a drunk husband who couldn't hold himself together during a two-hour event?

Everything escalated even further one early Saturday morning, our busiest day of the week. My wake-up call happened to be the same time as the last call at the nearby bars: 1:30 a.m. I had thirty minutes to get to the bakery and assume my position in front of the doughnut fryer.

I embraced the early mornings. My bakers started mixing and cutting the dough at midnight. By the time I arrived, they would have several racks of doughnuts proofing by the fryer. I couldn't waste any time—yeast waits for no one. I knew exactly how long it should take from the time the doughnut rings were cut from the giant sheets of brioche dough to the time they needed to be dipped in hot oil, which stops the rise.

Fry at just the right time and my doughnuts would be light and airy and win the usual enthusiastic praise from my lines of customers. Fry too soon and they would be dense and heavy. Fry too late and they would be flat and greasy. Not only would these last two scenarios disappoint my customers but also they could devastate my family: the loss of revenue would mean I could no longer put food on their dinner table.

My three children routinely snuggled in bed with me, but my husband usually left the house each night, and I never knew when he came home. I usually found him the next morning on the sofa, TV still on, candy wrappers covering the coffee table, a rotten smell in the air.

But I still needed him to take care of our children while I ran my bakery. That morning, I walked down the stairs to find all of the lights on and the couch empty.

I looked in every room, hoping he would be in one of them. I realized with mounting panic that I didn't have a back-up plan. I couldn't leave a four-, six-, and seven-year-old by themselves. But if I couldn't get to the bakery to fry the doughnuts, no one could do it for me. Every baker was already busy at work, and none of them knew how to fry.

My heart raced as I recalled the nights he didn't come home, the nights he slept in the van too drunk to find his way back. I called his phone. I could hear it ringing, but I couldn't tell where the sound was coming from—outside? I opened the front door.

There, on the porch, my husband sat a couple steps down, slumped over onto the railing. His phone was ringing through his back pocket. His greasy hair looked as if it hadn't been washed in days. He stunk of stale beer and cigarettes.

My panic turned to rage. He had an uncanny way of knowing how to completely derail me when I had a huge responsibility that needed to be my central focus. He also didn't like it when other people noticed my work. The more attention my doughnuts received, the more my husband sank into a dark, angry state.

I shook him until his eyes opened. He looked straight through me, blinking his eyes, tilting his head back, and spitting unintelligible words at me. I could feel my heart beating out of my chest.

He tried to steady himself on his feet and followed me up the stairs to the bedroom where the kids were still tucked under the covers. I swung the door closed, trying to prevent him from entering. He stuck his foot in the gap before I could shut it.

And then the rage started. He began screaming at me, clenching his fists tightly in front of his face and waving them in the air like he was preparing to throw a punch. I yelled back, pleading with him to stop.

The commotion woke up all three kids, and they were cowering under the blankets, sobbing. Josie's head poked out from under the sheet as she wept: "Daddy, please stop yelling at Mommy. You promised you wouldn't yell anymore. You promised."

It was one thing for him to pick a fight with me. But I couldn't protect the kids from watching their father turn into a monster in front of their eyes. Under the blankets, Keegan remained silent and still. I could see Mac's small body shaking. I had to take control of the situation.

"I'm leaving," I said. "I'm taking the kids with me."

"You don't have the right!" he screamed. "You fucking cunt. You fucking witch."

I turned to the kids and told them we were going to the bakery. In response, my husband took his cell phone and threw it straight at my head. I ducked out of the way and it slammed against the wall, shattering and leaving a hole in the plaster. The kids stuck themselves to my side, afraid to let an inch between us. My husband stood in our way. I persisted.

Finally, he let us out of the bedroom, but he followed us down the stairs to the car, shouting, "You fucking bitch. You nasty cunt. You can't take my kids."

We got into the car. I locked the doors behind us, and the crying stopped immediately. I told the kids they were going camping in the bakery. They were thrilled. They never got to be at the bakery when the doughnuts were frying.

My head pounding, I drove three blocks to Montclair Bread Company. I led the kids inside and up the stairs to my office. I laid out their sleeping bags on the ground that I had somehow managed to grab as we rushed out of the house. I turned a movie on for them on one of the computers.

I had saved my children. Now I needed to save my doughnuts.

I ran to the trays and touched the dough. It started to collapse under my finger; it couldn't hold its shape. The doughnuts were overproofed: the yeast was starting to crash.

I couldn't waste another second. I pushed two racks of dough into the walk-in fridge to slow down the proofing process and buy myself some time. I had to fry 2,000 doughnuts right away if I wanted to be able to pay my staff and feed my family.

I began placing doughnuts into the hot oil. They weren't perfect—you could see the recesses from my fingertips in the dough—but they would do. The bakers dipped them in glaze while they were still hot. I worked for hours, with no time to check on the kids.

The sun was beginning to rise at 5 a.m. when my friend Anne came to the bakery to meet me for our regular Saturday morning run. I had forgotten to text her to cancel, and the second I saw her, I burst into tears. My staff was shocked—they had never seen me cry.

Anne finished her run without me and then sent her mother to the bakery with craft supplies for the kids. They made jewelry, they made collages, they painted. The kids called it the best day ever.

Meanwhile, my husband had been texting me all morning to say he was sorry. I knew this would happen, and I knew that if I returned, I would have three weeks of a perfect husband and father before everything fell apart again.

But I was exhausted. With some guilt, I took the kids home. The next morning, as soon as the kids were awake, I loaded them into the car right away. From her booster seat in the back, Josie piped up with a question: "Are you and Daddy getting a divorce?"

I didn't know she knew that word. "What does 'divorce' mean?" I responded.

"Well, Daddy yells at you a whole lot, and maybe if you had your own place to live, you would be happier."

I envisioned someone treating my daughter the way my husband treated me.

On Monday morning, I called a divorce lawyer.

"Are you really ready for this?" he asked. "You have to be willing to lose everything—your kids, your business, your home."

I wasn't ready. I didn't have the strength to fight. I was afraid I couldn't manage on my own.

It took five more years before I rented an apartment across the street from my bakery and walked out with my children, the clothes on my back, what was left of my dignity, and the Vitamix blender I had worked so hard to buy.

I threw myself into creating new doughnuts for the bakery, which by then had moved to a new, larger headquarters. When Prince Harry married Meghan Markle, I put the flavors of their wedding cake into lemon elderflower doughnuts, topped with edible flowers. I made a sweet potato casserole doughnut for Thanksgiving, a birthday cake doughnut for the bakery's birthday, and a poop emoji doughnut after Donald Trump was elected president. I also made a series of International Women's Day doughnuts that included a tribute to Ruth Bader Ginsburg—my hands ached for hours after piping dissent collars on dozens of chocolate doughnuts, but it was worth it!

I began to realize that not only could I do this on my own but also I could actually be more successful without the negativity holding me back.

BRIOCHE DOUGH

Makes 8 brioche doughnuts (yum buns, cinnamon rolls, sticky buns, or fritters)

I worked long and hard on this custom brioche recipe that can be made and finished in one day, unlike classic brioche, which requires an overnight rise. I wanted to create a light, airy dough while retaining a rich, buttery flavor. My dough is easy to work with and very forgiving. Once you are comfortable working with this dough, there are endless possibilities.

3½ cups unbleached all-purpose flour
2 tablespoons sugar
1½ teaspoons instant yeast
1½ cups whole milk

1 large egg
1 teaspoon kosher salt
½ cup (1 stick) cold unsalted butter, cubed

Place the flour, sugar, yeast, milk, and egg into the bowl of a stand mixer fitted with a dough hook. Mix on low speed for 3 minutes, until the ingredients are combined and a dough ball begins to form. Add the salt and mix on medium speed for 8 to 10 minutes. While the dough is mixing, add cubes of the butter, one at a time. No need to wait for one piece to mix thoroughly before adding the next—they will incorporate before the dough is finished. When the dough is finished mixing, you should be able to stretch a small piece so thin you can almost see through it.

Using vegetable oil or cooking spray, grease a container with an airtight lid. Place the dough in the container, cover it with the lid, and let it rest for 30 minutes. Remove the lid, then use your hands to stretch and fold all four sides of the dough into the center, allowing them to overlap as if you were wrapping a present (see page xviii). Flip the dough so the seams are on the bottom and the folds do not unravel. Replace the lid and let rest another 30 minutes before proceeding with Classic Brioche Doughnuts (page 74), Yum Buns (page 91), Cinnamon Rolls (page 94), Sticky Buns (page 96), or Fritters (page 98).

CHOCOLATE BRIOCHE DOUGH

Follow the recipe as directed, but add ¼ cup cocoa powder, ¼ cup additional sugar, and 1 tablespoon strong coffee or espresso with the milk.

CARROT BRIOCHE DOUGH

Follow the recipe as directed, but replace the milk with carrot juice and add 1 cup finely grated carrot along with the juice.

APPLE CIDER BRIOCHE DOUGH

Follow the recipe as directed, but replace the milk with apple cider. I prefer unfiltered cider, but filtered will also work.

Milk Powder and Doughnuts

At the peak of the 2020 coronavirus pandemic, when the stores had been cleared of all the toilet paper, sanitizing wipes, and snack foods, our weekend dairy delivery didn't arrive. We would have to go through Saturday and Sunday doughnut production without milk. At this point, I was getting used to hearing "out of stock," but I wasn't prepared for this.

I knew I had a stash of milk powder I used for a recipe months ago. I decided to reconstitute it with water and use it in the brioche. I substituted an equal amount of the reconstituted powder milk for whole milk in the recipe. The next day, the doughnuts were the lightest and fluffiest they had ever been. They had a richness I was never able to capture before. I immediately called my friend, an expert in food science, to find out what happened. He told me there is a protein found in milk that inhibits yeast activity. In order to break down the protein, the milk must be heated to a certain temperature, then cooled to use in the dough. Milk powder does not contain this protein. It provides all the benefits of dairy in the dough while letting the yeast do its thing, unadulterated.

CLASSIC BRIOCHE DOUGHNUTS

Makes 8 doughnuts

I'll admit it: I have a two-doughnut-a-day habit. When the first doughnuts emerge from the fryer in the morning, puffy, full of air, with a bright ring around the center, I cannot look away. Too hot to hold onto for more than a few seconds, they get dunked in vanilla glaze, which encases them in sugary sweetness. Biting into that pillow of sweet, buttery, yeasty fried dough makes everything right in the world. Once you've experienced a hot, freshly glazed doughnut, nothing else will ever compare.

Before you begin, take a look at the doughnut variations in this chapter. The flavor you choose will determine how you cut and shape your dough. Glazes, fillings, and toppings should be prepared in advance, and some need to be applied while the doughnuts are still hot.

1 recipe Brioche Dough (page 72)
Flour, for dusting
Canola oil, for frying

Divide the dough into eight equal pieces. (Cut it in half, then in quarters, then into eighths. It's easier to eyeball halves than trying to cut single eighths off a giant lump of dough.)

Dust a large sheet pan with flour.

To form Classic-Style Doughnuts (Vanilla-Glazed, Apple Cider, Maple Bacon, Mocha): Use your thumb and forefinger to pinch a hole through the center of each dough ball. Carefully shimmy it open, turning the ball to make a wider hole in the center. Repeat with the remaining pieces of dough.

To form Filled-Style Doughnuts (Jelly, Nutella, Boston Cream): Roll each piece of dough into a loose ball. Repeat with the remaining pieces of dough.

To form Bull's-Eye-Style Doughnuts (Tres Leches, Strawberry Shortcake, Hot Chocolate): Cut through the center of the doughnut using a 1-inch round circle cutter. Do not remove the circle of dough. It will rise and fry as one piece. Repeat with the remaining pieces of dough.

No matter which method you choose, place the doughnuts onto a floured sheet pan, about 3 inches apart.

Slide the pan into an unscented kitchen-sized garbage bag and fold the opening under the pan to make an airtight proofing space for the doughnuts to rise. After about 60 minutes, remove the pan from the bag and poke the dough with your fingertip. If the dough comes back halfway, it's ready to fry. If it comes back all the way, so you can't see your fingerprint, it's not ready yet. In a 70° kitchen, doughnuts should take 60 to 90 minutes to rise.

Start gathering the tools for frying. You will need a spider, two wooden spoons, and a cooling rack or sheets of newspaper (which will suck the grease away from the hot doughnuts).

Pour about 3 inches of canola oil into a large pot. Heat the oil over medium-high heat, until it reaches 365°F.

Carefully place each doughnut in the oil. After 90 seconds, use the handle ends of the wooden spoons to flip the doughnuts over. Continue to fry for another 90 seconds. Using the spider, transfer the doughnuts to a cooling rack or newspaper. Be sure to place a tray under the rack to catch the excess oil. Repeat with the remaining dough.

Follow the directions for glazing or topping: some doughnuts need to be glazed while warm.

VANILLA-GLAZED DOUGHNUTS

Makes 8 doughnuts

**1 recipe Classic Brioche Doughnuts, cut in
Classic Style (page 74)**
1 recipe Vanilla Glaze (page 110)

While the doughnuts are still warm, dip the top of the doughnut into the glaze until it reaches the white rim around the sides. Pull it out of the glaze and let the excess drop off before returning it to the tray. Eat right away, these don't keep well.

APPLE CIDER DOUGHNUTS

Makes 8 doughnuts

1 recipe Classic Brioche Doughnuts, made
    with Apple Cider Brioche Dough,
    cut in Classic Style (page 74)

1 teaspoon ground cinnamon

1 cup sugar

While the doughnuts are still warm, toss them in cinnamon and sugar mixture. Eat right away, these
don't keep well.

TRES LECHES DOUGHNUTS

Makes 8 doughnuts

The email came from the Food Network in December 2013: "I'm writing to invite you to consider joining us on the second season of our reality TV series *Donut Showdown*. Your gourmet donuts have quite the reputation, and we'd love for you to bring that level of culinary pedigree to the show."

How could I say no? The first round of competition involved incorporating Twizzlers into a doughnut in thirty minutes or less—and we nailed that! In the final round, the theme was "Fiesta," and the ingredient was avocado. I knew we had a chance because we had a tres leches doughnut on our rotating menu. I had recently experimented with avocado ice cream, so I knew how to use the avocado in the whipped cream topping for the version I made on the show. After we won the show's grand prize, this doughnut became our bestseller and has never left our bakery's menu.

Tres Leches Filling
½ cup evaporated milk
½ cup sweetened condensed milk
½ cup heavy cream

1 recipe Classic Brioche Doughnuts, cut in Bull's-Eye Style (page 74)
1 recipe Vanilla Glaze (page 110)
1 recipe Whipped Cream (page 114)
8 maraschino cherries

Make the tres leches filling the night before you make the doughnuts. Stir the evaporated milk, sweetened condensed milk, and heavy cream together. Refrigerate for at least 8 hours or overnight.

Immediately after frying the doughnuts, carefully peel the top off the center piece of the doughnut. Do not remove the entire center, just the crust at the top. This will create an opening in the middle of the doughnut for the tres leches filling.

While the doughnut is still warm, dip the rim in vanilla glaze, then fill the opening in the center with with 1 tablespoon of tres leches filling using a small pitcher or ladle. As the doughnuts cool, they will absorb the liquid.

Once they are completely cooled, use a pastry bag and a #8 star tip to pipe a mound of whipped cream into the center of the doughnuts. If they are still warm, the whipped cream will melt. Don't feel like fussing with a piping bag? You can spoon the whipped cream onto the center of the doughnuts—they will taste the same no matter how they look.

Add a maraschino cherry on top! Eat right away, these don't keep well.

MAPLE BACON DOUGHNUTS

Makes 8 doughnuts

This doughnut first appeared on the menu for Father's Day in 2013 and is one of our most popular on social media.

1 recipe Classic Brioche Doughnuts, cut in
    Classic Style (page 74)

1 recipe Maple Glaze (page 113)
8 strips cooked bacon

Allow the doughnuts to cool completely before dipping in maple glaze. Break each strip of bacon into thirds and arrange on top of each doughnut. Eat right away, these don't keep well.

CARROT CAKE DOUGHNUTS

Makes 8 doughnuts

Most doughnut shops use a mix that only requires adding water and mixing. I created the carrot cake doughnut to show off our ability to create unique doughs using fresh ingredients.

1 recipe Classic Brioche Doughnuts, made with Carrot Brioche Dough, cut in Classic Style (page 74)

1 recipe Cream Cheese Glaze (page 113)
¼ recipe (½ layer) Mombo's Carrot Cake without frosting (page 5)

Allow the doughnuts to cool before dipping in the cream cheese glaze. Crumble the cake into bits and sprinkle on top of the doughnuts. Eat right away, these don't keep well.

STRAWBERRY SHORTCAKE DOUGHNUTS

Makes 8 doughnuts

The Strawberry Shortcake doughnut first appeared on our Mother's Day menu. We loved it so much we kept it until the last of the strawberries were harvested from our local fields.

1 recipe Classic Brioche Doughnuts, cut in Bull's-Eye Style (page 74)
1 recipe Strawberry Glaze (page 111)

3 tablespoons strawberry jam
1 recipe Whipped Cream (page 114)
4 fresh strawberries, halved, stems intact

Allow the doughnuts to cool before removing the top of the center cutout. Dip the rim of the bull's-eye in strawberry glaze. Place 1 teaspoon strawberry jam in the center well. Top with whipped cream and half of a fresh strawberry. Eat right away, these don't keep well.

HOT CHOCOLATE DOUGHNUTS

Makes 8 doughnuts

This doughnut appears on the menu every January to help us make it through the bitter cold New Jersey winters with a bit of chocolate cheer.

1 recipe Classic Brioche Doughnuts, made with Chocolate Brioche Dough, cut in Bull's-Eye Style (page 74)

1 recipe Chocolate Doughnut Glaze (page 108)

½ cup marshmallow fluff

1 recipe Whipped Cream (page 114)

Allow the doughnuts to cool before removing the top of the center cutout. Dip the rim of the bull's-eye in chocolate doughnut glaze. Place 1 tablespoon marshmallow fluff in the center well. Top with 1 tablespoon whipped cream. Eat right away, these don't keep well.

MOCHA DOUGHNUTS

Makes 8 doughnuts

There is no denying how much we LOVE our coffee partner, Think Coffee from Brooklyn, NY. This doughnut was originally created to highlight our relationship with them. Is there anything better than coffee AND doughnut in one bite?!

1 recipe Classic Brioche Doughnuts, made with Chocolate Brioche Dough, cut in Classic Style (page 74), or 1 recipe Chocolate Cake Doughnuts (page 103)

1 recipe Chocolate Doughnut Glaze, coffee variation (page 108)

Allow the doughnuts to cool completely before dipping in the coffee-chocolate glaze. Eat right away, these don't keep well.

BOSTON CREAM DOUGHNUTS

Makes 8 doughnuts

During family vacations, my dad and I would always fight over who got the Boston Cream Doughnut from the assorted dozen box. It was one of the first flavors I introduced at MBCo, using an old-fashioned cooked custard filling and a rich chocolate ganache glaze.

1 recipe Classic Brioche Doughnuts, cut in Filled Style (page 74)

1 recipe Pastry Cream (page 115)

1 recipe Chocolate Doughnut Glaze (page 108)

Allow the doughnuts to cool completely.

Use a butter knife to poke a hole in the side of the doughnut and wiggle it around to create a pocket in the center. Place the pastry cream in a piping bag or a resealable plastic bag with the corner snipped off. Insert the tip of the piping bag in the hole you made in the doughnut and squeeze the pastry cream into the center until you feel the doughnut get heavier and plump.

Dip the top of the doughnut into the chocolate glaze until it reaches the white ring on the side. Pull it out of the glaze and allow the excess to drip off before returning it to the tray. Eat right away, these don't keep well.

NUTELLA DOUGHNUTS

Makes 8 doughnuts

After school in France, I would sit at the small round table in the kitchen with my French family. Mama made tea while my host sisters and I tried to empty the jar of Nutella onto our thick slices of rich butter brioche. It was a contest to see who could pile the most on top of their bread. The Nutella doughnut brings me right back to that little table in St. Glen.

1 recipe Classic Brioche Doughnuts, cut in Filled Style (page 74)
1 cup hazelnut spread (such as Nutella)

1 cup confectioners' sugar
1 tablespoon cocoa powder

Allow the doughnuts to cool completely.

Use a butter knife to poke a hole in the side of the doughnut and wiggle it around to create a pocket in the center. Place the hazelnut spread in a piping bag or a resealable plastic bag with the corner snipped off. Insert the tip of the piping bag in the hole you made in the doughnut and squeeze the hazelnut spread into the center until you feel the doughnut get heavier and plump.

Mix the confectioners' sugar and cocoa powder together in a small bowl. Coat the doughnuts in the sugar mixture. Eat right away, these don't keep well.

JELLY DOUGHNUTS

Jelly doughnuts are only as good as the jelly inside!

1 recipe Classic Brioche Doughnuts, cut in Filled Style (page 74)

1 cup jelly
1 cup confectioners' sugar

Allow the doughnuts to cool completely.

Use a butter knife to poke a hole in the side of the doughnut and wiggle it around to create a pocket in the center. Place the jelly in a piping bag or a resealable plastic bag with the corner snipped off. Insert the tip of the piping bag in the hole you made in the doughnut and squeeze the jelly into the center until you feel the doughnut get heavier and plump.

Place the confectioners' sugar in a small bowl. Coat the doughnuts in the sugar mixture. Eat right away, these don't keep well.

Alternate Endings

One of my biggest jobs as a bakery owner is minimizing waste. As much as possible, by-products are turned into new products. The following recipes are the perfect examples of waste management ingenuity in action. At Montclair Bread Co., the classic doughnuts are cut with a ring cutter, which results in tiny circles cut from the hole and diamond-shaped lumps cut between the rings. We can't just re-roll these scraps into more doughnuts because they wouldn't be nearly as fluffy. Yum buns, cinnamon rolls, sticky buns, and fritters are all items we began making from doughnut scraps that would otherwise be thrown away. But they are so tasty and so popular with our customers that we now make extra dough just for them.

YUM BUNS

My mother is not a baker or a good cook. Her idea of cooking dinner was adding frozen mixed veggies to a packet of ramen noodles. But every now and then, she would attempt to pull off a recipe from scratch. Her cinnamon buns were one of her few big wins: a basic white dough that was topped with cinnamon and sugar. I slathered mine in butter and ate them when they were still hot. I can count on one hand the number of times she made these, but I will never forget how comforting those little rolls were.

One morning at the bakery, I had a lot of dough scraps, and I decided to make some treats for the staff. The resulting buns, though much bigger and fluffier than the ones from my childhood, brought me right back to my mother's kitchen and the comfort I felt when eating her cinnamon buns. My daughter, Josie, loved them, too. We knew they had to be on our menu, but we couldn't figure out what to call them. Morning buns? Cinnamon swirls? Coffee buns? It was Josie who nailed it: yum buns!

1 recipe Classic Brioche Dough (page 72)
1 cup dark brown sugar
3½ teaspoons ground cinnamon, divided

1½ cups granulated sugar
1 cup (2 sticks) unsalted butter, melted

Turn the dough out on a floured work surface and roll into a 12 by 6-inch rectangle. In a small bowl, mix the brown sugar and 2 teaspoons of the cinnamon. Sprinkle the cinnamon-sugar mixture evenly across the surface of the dough.

Working from the long side of the rectangle, tuck and roll the dough, creating a log. Using the heel of your palm, press down to seal the seam all the way across the log. Using a serrated knife, cut the log in half, widthwise. Then cut the halves in half and the quarters in half, creating eight equal pieces.

Grease a muffin tin with cooking spray. Place each piece of dough into a muffin cup so that the swirl side (either one) faces up. It's okay if you have to smush the edges to tuck it into the pan. Cover the tin and let the dough rise for 1 to 2 hours, until the dough is cresting out of the cups and roughly doubled in size.

Preheat the oven to 350°F. Uncover the dough. Bake for 20 minutes, rotating the pan halfway through, until the tops of the buns are deep golden brown.

continued

While the buns are baking, mix the sugar and the remaining 1½ teaspoons cinnamon in a medium bowl. In a second medium bowl, melt the butter.

When the buns are finished baking, flip the muffin tin over to release them onto a work surface. While they are still warm, dip them in the butter, coating all sides. Hold each bun over the bowl of butter and allow any excess butter to drip off before coating it in the cinnamon-sugar mixture. Make sure to coat the whole exterior of the bun. Repeat with the remaining buns.

You do not have to wait for these to cool before you eat them. In fact, please eat them while they are warm to maximize the yum potential! These will keep wrapped airtight in the fridge for up to 2 days. Super dirty secret? I pop them in the microwave for 30 seconds to refresh them before eating them because they are so much better warm!

CINNAMON ROLLS

Makes 8 rolls

If you master this recipe, you will have the perfect show-stopping brunch addition for years to come. Who doesn't love a warm, gooey, cinnamon-y bun? It takes some patience to go through the process and give them time to rise, but they are well worth the wait and, unlike most recipes, you don't have to wait for them to cool before slathering them with cream cheese frosting. In fact, glazing them while they're still hot allows the frosting to melt down into the crevices of the swirls and makes them even more indulgent.

1 recipe Classic Brioche Dough (page 72)
1 cup brown sugar

2 teaspoons ground cinnamon
1 recipe Cream Cheese Frosting (page 113)

Turn the dough out onto a floured work surface and roll into a 12 by 6-inch rectangle. In a small bowl, mix the brown sugar and cinnamon together. Sprinkle the cinnamon-sugar mixture evenly across the surface of the dough.

Starting with the long side of the rectangle, tuck and roll the dough, creating a log. Using the heel of your palm, press down to seal the seam all the way across the log. Using a serrated knife, cut the log in half, widthwise. Then cut the halves in half and the quarters in half, creating eight equal pieces.

Grease a 9 by 13-inch baking pan using cooking spray. Place the buns, swirl side up, in the pan, spaced evenly apart. Cover the pan and let the dough rise for 1 to 2 hours. The buns should fill up the space between them so they're all touching.

Preheat the oven to 350°F.

Uncover the dough. Bake for 25 to 30 minutes, until the tops of the buns are deep golden brown.

I recommend frosting the buns while they're still warm so that the frosting melts into the creases and folds of the buns. But if you prefer the frosting to stay fluffy on top of the buns, wait until they cool completely. These will keep wrapped airtight at room temperature for up to 2 days.

NOTE: If you want to avoid setting your alarm for 4 a.m. to have these breakfast-ready, prepare the buns the night before: Place them in the pan. Slide the pan in an unscented kitchen-sized garbage bag, or tightly cover it with plastic wrap, and refrigerate overnight. After you remove the pan from the fridge, the buns will need to rise at room temperature for 2 hours before you can bake and frost them.

STICKY BUNS

Makes 8 buns

Brad's father, Sol, frequently sends me notes about different bakeries he's visited, pizzas he's tried, and recipes he thinks I would like to use. For months he asked me whether I had a good sticky bun recipe. He ranks his favorite bakeries by their sticky buns. Finally, I caved and made Sol a tray of cinnamon-pecan sticky buns. He loved them, and so did my bakery team. We even put them on our weekend menu.

Use a 9 by 13-inch metal baking pan for this recipe: it will be harder to flip the baked buns if you use a glass or ceramic pan.

2 cups dark brown sugar, firmly packed, divided

½ cup (1 stick) unsalted butter

½ cup heavy cream

½ cup honey

2 cups chopped nuts and raisins, divided (optional; I like pecans, walnuts, and sliced almonds)

1 recipe Classic Brioche Dough (page 72)

2 teaspoons ground cinnamon

Warm 1 cup of the brown sugar and the butter in a medium saucepan over low heat, stirring, until smooth and shiny. Remove from the heat and stir in the heavy cream and honey.

Pour the mixture into a 9 by 13-inch metal pan and let cool. Sprinkle 1 cup of the nuts over the liquid.

Turn the dough out on a floured work surface and roll into a 12 by 6-inch rectangle. In a small bowl, mix the remaining 1 cup brown sugar and cinnamon together. Sprinkle the cinnamon-sugar mixture evenly across the surface of the dough. If you are using nuts and raisins, sprinkle the remaining 1 cup on top of the cinnamon-sugar mix.

Starting with the long side of the rectangle, tuck and roll the dough, creating a log. Using the heel of your palm, press down to seal the seam all the way across the log. Using a serrated knife, cut the log in half, widthwise. Then cut the halves in half and the quarters in half, creating eight equal pieces.

Place the rolls, cut side up, evenly spaced, in the pan on top of the liquid base. Cover the pan and let the dough rise for 1 to 2 hours or until the rolls take up all the space in the pan and touch each other.

Preheat the oven to 350°F.

Bake for 30 to 40 minutes, until the buns are dark brown on top and the liquid starts to bubble up the edges of the pan. Cool for 10 minutes. Then flip the pan of buns upside down onto a sheet pan. Carefully lift the pan straight up to reveal your buns. These will keep wrapped airtight at room temperature for up to 2 days.

FRITTERS

Makes 12 fritters

Classic doughnut fritters are made with chopped dough and fruit. When I tried to make these, too much fruit worked its way out of the dough and was lost in the fryer. So I devised this cinnamon-roll-style fritter, which ensures that all the fruit stays in the doughnut. I never use sugar in the raw dough. If sugar gets into the frying oil, it blackens and sticks to the sides of the pan.

1 recipe Classic Brioche Dough (page 72)
2 teaspoons ground cinnamon
2 cups fresh fruit, thinly sliced (apples, bananas, pears, or peaches)

Flour, for dusting
Vegetable oil, for frying
1 recipe Vanilla Glaze (page 110)

Turn the dough out on a floured work surface and roll into a 12 by 5-inch rectangle. Sprinkle the cinnamon across the dough. Evenly distribute the fruit slices across the dough surface. Starting with the long side of the rectangle, tuck and roll the dough, creating a log. Using the heel of your palm, press down to seal the seam all the way across the log. Using a serrated knife, cut the log in half, widthwise. Then cut the halves in half and the quarters in half, creating eight equal pieces.

Liberally flour a baking sheet. Place the dough pieces on the sheet, 3 inches apart. Cover the pan with an unscented kitchen-sized garbage bag and let the dough rise for 2 hours at room temperature.

Heat 2 inches of oil in a wide, shallow pot over medium-high heat until it reaches 365°F.

Carefully drop each piece of dough into the oil. Fry for about 80 seconds on each side, until the fritters are fluffy and browned on each side. Use the ends of wooden spoons to flip the doughnuts in the oil. Using a spider, transfer the doughnuts to a cooling rack.

Glaze while still warm. Eat right away, these don't keep well.

VANILLA BUTTERMILK CAKE DOUGHNUTS

Makes 18 doughnuts (12 round, 8 stick-shaped)

I was never one for cake doughnuts. I never tried to make them and didn't care to eat them. I'll take my yeasty glazed and be on my way. In 2014, I took a doughnut-making workshop with Jory Downer of the acclaimed Bennison's Bakery in Evanston, Illinois, and he shared this recipe for Buttermilk Cake Doughnuts. I could not stop eating them!!! They were not too sweet and had a firmer texture than most cake doughnuts I had tried before. I put them on the Montclair Bread Co. menu immediately. I've made several versions of them since, but this is where it all started—a basic vanilla-glazed buttermilk cake doughnut.

1 recipe Vanilla Glaze (page 110)	1½ tablespoons baking powder
Vegetable oil, for frying	½ teaspoon baking soda
¼ cup shortening (such as Crisco)	½ teaspoon kosher salt
½ cup sugar	1½ cup buttermilk
1 large egg	1 tablespoon vanilla extract or bourbon
3 cups all-purpose flour	

These must be glazed while still warm, so make your glaze first.

Heat about 2 inches of oil in a wide, shallow pot over medium-high heat to 365°F.

In the bowl of a stand mixer fitted with a paddle attachment, cream the shortening and sugar together on medium-high speed until combined. Add the egg and mix until it is fluffy.

In a medium bowl, combine the flour, baking powder, baking soda, and salt.

In a small bowl, stir together the buttermilk and vanilla.

continued

Add half of the flour mixture to the shortening mixture and mix together on low speed until incorporated. Add half of the buttermilk and mix until incorporated. Repeat with the remaining flour mixture and buttermilk, mixing just until incorporated. Do not overmix: no one wants a chewy cake doughnut.

Turn the dough out on a floured work surface and sprinkle more flour on top of the dough. Use a floured rolling pin to roll the dough ½ inch thick. Cut the doughnuts using two ring cutters, 3.5 inch for the outer circle and 1 inch for the center. If you don't have ring cutters, you can use the rim of a glass for the outer edge and the wide part of a piping tip for the center. Knock the flour off the scraps and roll them together into a 3 by 8-inch rectangle. Cut strips of dough 1 inch wide.

Gently drop the doughnuts and strips into the hot oil. Time them: 60 seconds on each side. Use the end of a wooden spoon to flip them over. Transfer the doughnuts to newspaper or paper towels to drain. Glaze while warm! Eat right away, these don't keep well.

Variations

CHOCOLATE CAKE
Replace 3 cups of flour with 2¾ cups flour and add ¼ cup cocoa powder; replace the vanilla extract with strong coffee.

PUMPKIN CAKE
Replace 1½ cups buttermilk with 1 cup buttermilk and ½ cup canned pumpkin purée; replace 1 tablespoon vanilla with 1 tablespoon pumpkin pie spice.

GINGERBREAD CAKE
Omit the vanilla and add 2 tablespoons blackstrap molasses, ¼ teaspoon ground cloves, 1 tablespoon ground ginger, ½ teaspoon ground cinnamon, and ¼ teaspoon ground nutmeg.

POTATO DONUTS

Makes 12 donuts

Yes, these are donuts, not doughnuts. This was my grandmother Mombo's recipe, so I'm keeping the spelling the way she wrote it. Her recipe didn't have a measurement for flour; it just says "add flour to make soft sticky dough," which is also the last instruction on her card. Luckily, I spent enough time watching her and working with her in the kitchen to know exactly what she meant, and I've filled in the gaps for you. If you like an "Old-Fashioned"-style doughnut, the kind that bursts and splits to create caverns for the glaze to settle into, this is the recipe for you.

1 cup plain mashed potatoes (with no dairy or seasonings—not leftover from dinner!)

1 cup sugar

1 tablespoon unsalted butter, melted

½ cup whole milk

1 large egg

2½ cups all-purpose flour

1 tablespoon baking powder

¼ teaspoon ground nutmeg

6 to 8 cups nonhydrogenated vegetable shortening or canola oil

1 recipe Vanilla Glaze (page 110) or Brown Sugar Glaze (page 33)

In a large bowl, whisk together the potatoes, sugar, butter, milk, and egg. Add the flour, baking powder, and nutmeg; stir until a dough forms.

In a large, wide pot, heat about 3 inches of shortening or oil over medium-high heat to 350°F.

On a floured work surface, using a floured rolling pin, gently roll the dough ½ inch thick (that's about to the top knuckle on your pointer finger). Use as much flour as you need to prevent sticking. Using any concentric circle cutters, cut the donuts. If you don't have ANYTHING round, you can cut strips of dough and fry dunking sticks!

Carefully drop each piece of dough into the hot oil. Fry for about 80 seconds on each side, until the donuts are fluffy and browned on each side. Use the ends of wooden spoons to flip the doughnuts in the oil. Transfer to paper towels or newspaper to drain.

Glaze while still warm. Eat right away, these don't keep well.

Variation

SWEET POTATO
Use sweet potatoes instead of regular potatoes, increase the flour to 3 cups, and use ground ginger in place of nutmeg.

Tools to use in place of proper circle cutters and rolling pins

Cut circles with:
   Mason jar lids
   The top of a water glass
   The wide end of a piping tip
   A biscuit cutter

Roll dough with:
   A wine bottle
   A wooden dowel
   A mason jar
   A glass water bottle

CRULLERS/CHURROS

French crullers and Mexican churros start with the same dough, a traditional pâte à choux. "Chou" means "cabbage" in French. When this dough, "pâte," is baked or fried, it puffs up like a big cabbage. Using a star-shaped piping tip gives both of these doughnuts their ridges, which help to hold their glaze or sugar topping. Once they're fried, the centers are almost hollow. They are as light as air thanks to the abundance of eggs in the recipe.

½ cup whole milk

½ cup water

½ cup (1 stick) unsalted butter

1½ cups all-purpose flour

5 large eggs

Vegetable oil, for frying

1 recipe Honey Glaze (page 112) or another glaze, for crullers

2 cups sugar, for churros

2 teaspoons ground cinnamon, for churros

Chocolate Dipping Sauce

1⅔ cups milk of your choice (I like coconut milk)

1 cup semisweet chocolate chips

1 teaspoon ground cinnamon

1 teaspoon vanilla extract

Pinch of ground cayenne pepper

Heat the milk, water, and butter in a medium saucepan over medium-high heat; bring to a boil, stirring occasionally. Add the flour and stir until a dough ball forms. Cook for 2 minutes more to remove the starch, stirring occasionally. A film should form on the bottom of the pot.

Transfer the dough to the bowl of a stand mixer fitted with a paddle attachment. Add the eggs one at a time, mixing on medium speed in between, until incorporated. The dough will start to break apart and look like a terrible mess. Don't fret. It will come back together. Keep mixing until it starts to resemble smooth, goopy paste.

Place the dough in a pastry bag with a large star tip or a resealable plastic bag with the corner snipped.

Heat about 2 inches of vegetable oil in a wide pot over medium-high heat to 365°F.

To make crullers, lay a large piece of parchment paper out on a work surface and pipe 3½-inch circles onto the paper, about 2 inches apart. Use scissors to cut the paper around each cruller. Place each paper, doughnut side down, into the oil. Use a wooden spoon to press down on the paper so it dips under the oil and releases from the dough. Immediately fish the paper out with the spoon.

Fry for 2 minutes on each side, until deep brown and puffy. The crullers will split open in places and expand. Using a spider, remove from the pot and dip immediately into honey glaze. Eat right away, these don't keep well.

To make churros, mix the sugar and cinnamon together in a wide, shallow bowl; set aside.

Pipe 4 to 6-inch lengths of dough directly into the hot oil, using a paring knife to cut the dough off from the piping tip. Allow them to fully submerge in the oil and fry for 2 minutes. The dough will puff and brown slightly. Use tongs or wooden spoons to rotate the churros so the sides brown evenly. When the churros are deep brown and puffy, remove them from the oil and immediately dip them into the cinnamon-sugar mixture. Dredge the churros until they are completely coated.

To make the chocolate dipping sauce, heat the milk to a simmer in a saucepan over low heat. Add the chocolate chips, cinnamon, vanilla, and cayenne to a medium bowl. Pour the hot milk over the chocolate and spices. Let the bowl sit for 1 minute, then whisk the ingredients together until they are smooth and shiny. Serve warm with the churros. Eat right away, these don't keep well.

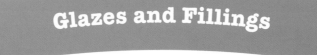

CHOCOLATE GLAZE

Makes about 1 cup, or enough to glaze about 8 doughnuts

1 cup heavy cream
½ cup semisweet chocolate chips
1 teaspoon vanilla extract

Heat the heavy cream in a small saucepan over medium heat until it comes to a simmer, watching carefully so it does not boil and scorch the bottom of the pot.

Place the chocolate chips into a small heatproof bowl. Pour the hot cream over the chocolate. Let sit for 1 minute before stirring together; stir until the chocolate melts.

Stir in the vanilla. Place the glaze in a wide, shallow bowl.

Variations

MEXICAN CHOCOLATE
Add ½ teaspoon ground cinnamon and ¼ teaspoon chili powder.

NONDAIRY
Substitute coconut milk for the heavy cream.

COFFEE
Add ¼ cup coarse-ground coffee to the heavy cream. Substitute ¾ cup white chocolate chips for the semisweet chips. Strain the cream to remove any coffee grounds before adding to the chocolate; it's okay if some grounds remain.

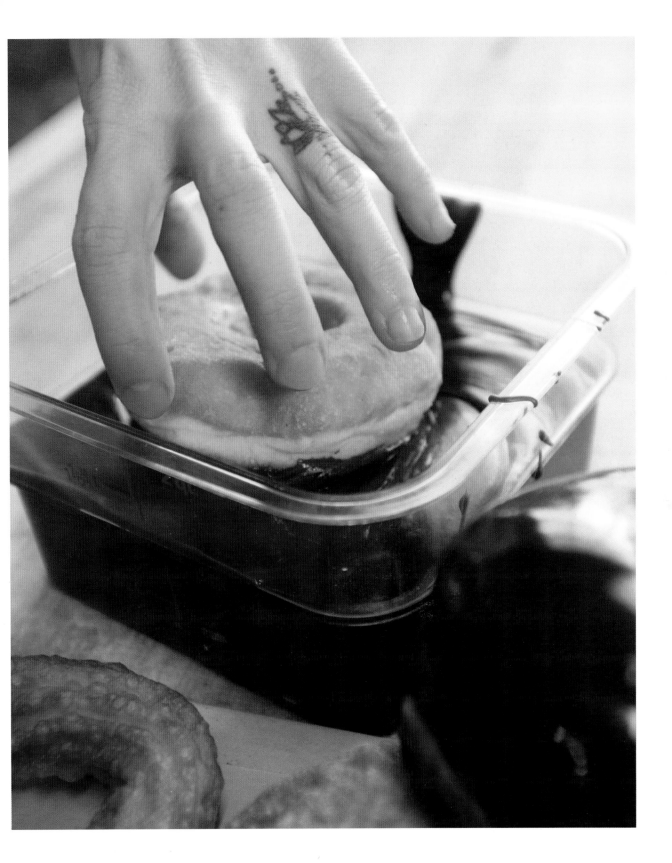

VANILLA GLAZE

Makes 1½ cups, or enough to glaze 8 to 12 Classic Brioche Doughnuts

1 cups confectioners' sugar
½ teaspoon light corn syrup
Seeds scraped from ½ vanilla bean
   or 1 teaspoon vanilla extract

Pinch of kosher salt
2 tablespoons warm water, divided

Combine the sugar, corn syrup, vanilla, and salt in a medium bowl. Slowly whisk 1 tablespoon of the water, making a paste, to beat all the lumps out of the sugar. Gradually add the remaining 1 tablespoon water and whisk until smooth and thin enough to glaze.

Place the glaze in a wide, shallow bowl.

STRAWBERRY/FRUIT GLAZE

Makes about 1 cup, or enough to glaze about 8 doughnuts

1 cup confectioners' sugar

1 tablespoon strawberry jam (you can use any fruit jam or purée)

Pinch of kosher salt

1 to 2 tablespoons warm water

Place the sugar, jam, and salt into a small bowl. Gradually whisk in the water, 1 tablespooon at a time, making a paste, to beat all the lumps out of the sugar. If the glaze is thick and pasty, slowly add more water, 1 teaspoon at a time, and whisk until it is smooth and thin enough to glaze.

Place the glaze in a wide, shallow bowl.

HONEY GLAZE

Makes about 1 cup, or enough to glaze about 8 crullers

1 cup confectioners' sugar

1 tablespoon honey

Pinch of kosher salt

1 to 2 tablespoons warm water

Place the sugar, honey, and salt in a small bowl. Gradually whisk in the water, 1 tablespoon at a time, making a paste, to beat all the lumps out of the sugar. If the glaze is thick and pasty, slowly add more water, 1 teaspoon at a time, and whisk until it is smooth and thin enough to glaze.

Place the glaze in a wide, shallow bowl.

MAPLE GLAZE

Makes about 1 cup, or enough to glaze about 8 doughnuts

½ cup brown sugar, firmly packed

½ cup maple syrup

¼ cup whole milk

¼ cup unsalted butter

½ teaspoon vanilla extract

Pinch of kosher salt

Heat all the ingredients in a medium saucepan over medium heat. Bring to a boil and allow to bubble for 2 minutes, then transfer to the bowl of a stand mixer fitted with a whisk attachment. Beat at low speed until cool, about 10 minutes. The mixture should have the consistency of caramel.

Place the glaze in a wide, shallow bowl.

CREAM CHEESE GLAZE

Makes 2 cups, or enough to glaze 8 to 12 doughnuts

4 ounces cream cheese, at room
  temperature

½ teaspoon ground cinnamon

1 recipe Vanilla Glaze (page 110)

In the bowl of a stand mixer fitted with a paddle attachment, cream the cream cheese on medium-high speed until light and fluffy, about 3 minutes. Add the cinnamon and beat until incorporated. Slowly add the vanilla glaze to the cream cheese and blend until smooth and completely combined.

Place the glaze in a wide, shallow bowl.

CREAM CHEESE FROSTING

½ cup (1 stick) unsalted butter, at room
   temperature
4 ounces cream cheese, at room
   temperature

3 cups confectioners' sugar
1 teaspoon vanilla extract

In the bowl of a stand mixer fitted with a paddle attachment, cream the butter and cream cheese on medium-high speed until combined. Add the confectioners' sugar and vanilla. Mix on low until the sugar is incorporated, then mix on high for 5 to 6 minutes, until the frosting is light and fluffy.

WHIPPED CREAM

2 cups heavy cream
½ cup confectioners' sugar

1 teaspoon vanilla extract

In the bowl of a stand mixer fitted with a whisk attachment, beat the heavy cream, confectioners' sugar, and vanilla on medium speed until firm peaks form, about 3 minutes. Don't overmix or you will end up with sweet butter. It's okay to periodically stop the mixer and check to see whether the cream can hold a peak. In other words, it should have clearly defined ridges that do not sink back into the cream when you stop the mixer.

PASTRY CREAM

Makes about 2 cups

Timing is crucial with this recipe. Before you start, gather all of the ingredients, as well as a medium pot, whisk, mixing bowl, spatula, fine mesh metal strainer, and sheet pan.

2 cups whole milk, divided
½ cup sugar, divided
2 tablespoons cornstarch

2 large egg yolks
1½ teaspoons unsalted butter
1 teaspoon vanilla extract

Heat 1½ cups of the milk and ¼ cup of the sugar in a medium saucepan over medium heat, stirring occasionally, until it starts to bubble. Stir occasionally so it doesn't scald. Whisk in the cornstarch, the remaining ¼ cup sugar, and egg yolks. Add the remaining ½ cup milk a little at a time until the mixture is thin and smooth.

Pour the mixture through a strainer into a mixing bowl, then return it back to the saucepan and heat it over medium heat. Stir until it starts to boil—keep it moving or you will end up with scrambled eggs. When it starts to pop, remove it from the heat. Stir in the butter and vanilla. Pour the custard onto a sheet pan and cover with plastic wrap.

Refrigerate until cool.

So You Want to Open a Bakery?

Every so often, I get notes from people who want to open their own bakery. Sometimes it's because they baked a batch of cupcakes and all the party guests raved. Often, it's someone who wants to leave the corporate world for what they see as a fun job that can't be too hard, right? One day, I received an email from one such person. He thought having a bakery would be great; he could still take lots of vacations, his wife could pursue other interests, and they wouldn't be "dough-deep" in the business.

Here's how I wanted to reply:

Have you ever baked anything? Do you have your own recipes? Can you use the recipes to make 1,000 times what you would make at home . . . every day? Can you also make 1,000 of thirty other items and have everything ready when you open at 6 a.m.? Do you have a summer and winter version of each of your recipes to account for the changes in temperature and humidity? Did you know that's a thing?

About that 6 a.m. thing . . . how much do you value sleep? Is three hours per night good for you? Are you comfortable starting your day at 12:01 a.m.? It counts as early morning because it's technically a.m., right?

When was the last time you stood on your feet for ten to fourteen hours without a break to sit down? Are you confident you can maintain this amount of time on your feet for six to twelve days straight?

Do your meals have to be eaten while hot? Are you comfortable substituting cold snacks for hot meals? You will have about five minutes three or four times each day to eat whatever you can reach.

Do you have a significant amount of money in savings or a wealthy partner to supplement your income? How long can you go without a paycheck? Do you plan on having staff to help you run the bakery? Do you plan to pay them more than the standard going rate so they'll continue to work for you?

Do you like the smell of baked goods? Do you like it when your clothes smell like baked goods? How about your car? Your house? Your kids' clothes? ALL.THE.TIME?

Do you have kids? Are they comfortable losing one parent? How will you respond to the notes from the teachers asking why you were the only parent who wasn't present at your child's super important book reading?

How gullible are your kids? Can you easily convince them that Christmas is December 26? How about Easter Monday? Thanksgiving Friday? Do they really care if you miss their birthdays? How important are family weddings to you? Will anyone in your family hold a grudge if you miss a funeral, or five?

Do you have a lot of friends? Do they invite you to dinners, drinks, and other evening or weekend activities? Do you think they'll still be your friends if you decline every invitation for the next [how many years you plan on having your bakery open] years?

Can you cover multiple employees who call out on the same day? On three hours of sleep?

Do you like people? Do you like people who complain about the baked goods you just spent the last ten to fourteen hours on your feet to make for them?

Can you make a doughnut look like a stiletto-heeled shoe? Can you make a cake for 250 people with an hour's notice, even if you don't plan to have cakes on your menu? Can you make a gluten-free, vegan version of everything on your menu? Do you plan to be peanut-free? Tree nut-free? Egg-free? Dairy-free? Flavor-free? You know, there are a lot of people with a lot of restrictions who love bakeries! Can you fully stock your shelves five minutes before closing? Can you just make MORE??? Can you make it and sell it for less than Costco?

In addition to baking, do you have the following skills:

Barista	Legal	Arts & Crafts	Menu Development
Retail Management	Town Planning	Web Design	& Planning
Customer Service	Construction	Project Management	Health Safety/ServSafe
Marketing	Crisis Management	Interior Design	Sanitation
Public Relations	Auto Repair	Logistics	Food Writing
Bookkeeping	Sourcing & Purchasing	Facilities Management	Editing
Plumbing	Debt Collections	HVAC	Sales
Electrical	Banking	OSHA	
Accounting	Graphic Design	Human Resources	

If you're ready to take on these tasks, it is high time you open a bakery!

Do Not Buy a $3 Doughnut Cutter

There is nothing more frustrating than a cutter that doesn't cut. Cheap cutters often don't line up properly, making it nearly impossible to remove the hole from the center of the dough. The best cutters are made from forged steel and start at $75 each. You do not need a doughnut cutter to make a great doughnut.

CHAPTER 04

COMMUNITY FAVORITES

I didn't set out to launch a running club. But I was a little lonely. I was gaining weight from eating two doughnuts a day (one glazed, one apple cider—both hot from the fryer). And I was overwhelmed by the thought of making 4,000 doughnuts to celebrate 4,000 likes on our Facebook page.

So instead, we hosted a 4K race to celebrate—cobbled together in two weeks—with no starting line and no finish line. As I ran my first mile since high school gym class, I quickly discovered that running was the only time I could have an uninterrupted adult conversation. The phone wasn't ringing to alert me of the latest bakery emergency. The kids weren't tugging at my legs for attention. I was able to clear my head and have a linear thought. Most importantly, for the first time, I was making friends who had no idea I owned a bakery and required nothing of me except a partner to help them through the run.

Running made me feel in control, even when the rest of my life felt out of control.

When four friends and I got together to launch the first Fueled by Doughnuts group run, we sat around talking about what was desirable about running with a group and what felt uneasy. We agreed that there was nothing worse than showing up to run with a group only to be left behind the pack. So we decided that we would always ensure that no one ran alone, no matter how fast they were running. We wanted to always acknowledge new runners

and introduce them to everyone. We never wanted our runs to stray more than three miles from a water fountain. We would come up with routes that could be easily cut off at three miles and then again at eight miles, and we would run through as much of Montclair as we could. We would always start with a group photo and end with doughnuts.

In short, we would focus on people first. Running second.

When the town pushed back on our next run, a Baker's Dozen Half Marathon, after it had already sold out and when I was sick with pneumonia, I pulled myself out of bed to stalk the mayor at a local ribbon cutting to convince him otherwise.

Our runs became so frequent that after a year of them—just twelve months after I had run my first mile since high school—I was able to run the New York City marathon. I was also able to run six miles through Brooklyn on a first date with the man who would become my partner, Brad Barket. Not only did he eventually become my live-in running partner but also he taught me how to laugh again and helped me rediscover my passion for baking.

Brad later moved to Montclair and became involved in the running club. Our membership grew to 2,000 members, who come for five runs a week and a monthly pizza party. Our two annual runs consistently sell out in less than an hour.

My life had turned around.

Then one day in 2018, it almost ended.

I zoomed through the tree-lined streets of West Orange, a neighboring town, with my friend Yana. We were preparing for the Lake Placid Ironman in a month, a race that meant a lot to me because I worked hard over the last two years to overcome my fear of swimming and biking to complete the trifecta.

I hadn't slept much the night before. After a week of intense training, every push and pull of the pedals took effort. Our water bottles were empty. We hit every single traffic light in the last two miles of our ride. I didn't want to stop for another one. We hit a slight slope and saw another light ahead. Yana and I peddled faster to avoid the red light. She was about to pass a forest-green minivan when the driver opened the door in front of her. She swerved, gracefully avoiding it.

As I prepared to do the same, a man got out of the van and stood beside it. I struggled to get around him, too. I hit my brake, and my bike fishtailed on the damp pavement. I couldn't get control of it. In seconds, the wobbling stopped, and I felt my wheels slip out from under me.

My left hip slammed on the pavement, in the middle of a busy intersection, taking the full brunt of my fall. I screamed. I couldn't move. My bike was on top of me, my feet still locked into the pedals. I felt someone take my hand. I could see Yana standing over me. I reached for my phone in the pocket on the back of my jersey. I texted Brad. "There was an accident."

Yana grabbed the phone out of my hand and called Brad. She was yelling into the phone. I was in pain, but I didn't know where it was coming from. I was afraid to look down for fear of what I would see. I could hear sirens. Someone had called an ambulance. The cops arrived first. An officer was standing next to me. I held onto her calf and begged her not to leave.

The paramedics arrived. They unhooked my shoes from the pedals and lifted the bike off. They wouldn't let me remove my helmet. They put a brace around my neck and brought over two boards to slide under me. The boards met in the middle and pinched the skin on my back. I cried out. I recognized the medic: he was one of my customers at the bakery. He thought I was delirious.

A harrowing nine hours after I arrived at the hospital, I was visited by an orthopedic surgeon. He had bad news. My injury required surgery. The force of the crash's impact sent the ball of my hip straight into the socket, which pulverized the bone. My suspicion that my hip was dislocated was correct, but it was even worse than I had imagined: the socket no longer existed.

The doctor told me this particular fracture, known as "acetabular," is rare. It typically happens only in high-impact accidents, such as car crashes and competitive cycling. The doctor told me this injury could have killed me. The chances of a patient with an acetabular fracture dying from internal bleeding are high. Brad was with me throughout this whole terrible conversation. But it had become very clear that sitting by my hospital bedside was the last place he wanted to be. We were both used to being fiercely independent, totally in control of our own lives. Neither one of us was a caretaker, and that's what brought us together.

I thought about all the times I had to be brave in front of my kids so they wouldn't be afraid. I thought about the time I held Josie's hand while the doctors stitched the cut above her eye she got from falling into the coffee table. I told her it would all be over soon; she just had to relax and let the doctors do their jobs. Now it was my turn to let someone else be in control.

The eight-hour surgery produced a fourteen-inch incision and took two metal plates, twelve screws, and one giant pin to reconstruct my pelvis. I lost a lot of blood. They had to give me transfusions on the operating table. They told me not to bear any weight on my left side for at least six weeks and that I would be lucky to start running again in six months.

The running club, alerted to the hospital's lack of food, began organizing a meal train. One runner friend, Gina, brought my kids to visit me for the first time since the accident. I was so happy to see them. But at the same time, I felt a tremendous sense of guilt for causing them to worry about the unknown. We had just lost my grandmother Mombo a few months before. Now the kids looked at me below the bandages and catheter and IVs and were convinced I was going to die, too.

Josie, then ten, didn't want to leave my side. Mac, six, thought all the tubes were funny, especially the one that held my pee. Keegan, eight, stayed off to the side, internalizing everything. They had never seen me in a vulnerable state. I rarely got sick or hurt, and when I did, I always kept everything under control. They wanted to know when I could walk, when I could come home, when I would get my stitches out. I wanted to know, too.

Runner friends kept trickling in, brushing my hair, delivering chocolate-covered strawberries and coloring books and bags of cleansing wipes. Over the next several months, as I recovered and learned to walk again, they brought home-cooked meals every day. Five months later, when I ran our race well ahead of doctors' predictions, they cheered me on, along with the governor of New Jersey.

A year after the accident, with the support of my medical team, I raced the Wineglass Marathon to a six-minute personal best and qualified for the competitive Boston Marathon.

During the worst part of this, when people told me "What doesn't kill you makes you stronger" and "Life only gives you what you can handle," I wanted to punch them in the face. I know they meant well, but it was so hard to hear when I needed my ten-year-old to help me put my socks on.

I am no stranger to letdowns. I understand what it's like to have life put on hold and not know what the future looks like. The unknown is the worst part. What can we hang on to? What hope is still alive?

But then I see our patio filled with customers eating pizza. Then I see a grandfather bringing in a tiny girl for muffins. Then I watch my staff creating trays of fluffy glazed doughnuts. That's when I know hope is alive.

It's about people first. Food second.

PIZZA

Makes two 12-inch pizzas or one 9 by 13-inch focaccia

Amazingly, one can work in a bakery yet find nothing to eat when starving. When I worked at the Patisserie in Milford, Pennsylvania, I discovered that if I refrigerated extra focaccia dough overnight, the lumps of old dough made great pizza crust. Using the dough to make focaccia the day it is mixed yields a thick, airy crust that can be topped with a few fresh slices of tomato and basil leaves. When the dough is refrigerated overnight, it can stretch ten times its size into a thin, crisp pizza crust.

Flash forward two decades to Montclair Bread Company. The first time I made pizza in my bakery space was from leftovers and entirely to feed my staff. When we started the running club, I mixed focaccia dough to use for pizzas served at our leadership team meetings. In between meetings, we plotted the toppings: our favorites included such delectable combinations as sweet potato, blue cheese, and bacon, and asparagus, corn, and ricotta. Eventually, the running club leaders were making their own pizzas, and we had so much fun that we opened up pizza-making to the general public. After that, our outdoor patio became a destination, complete with a wood-fired oven and live Friday night music—and the best pizza I've ever baked.

2 cups cool tap water
1 teaspoon instant yeast
4 cups all-purpose flour
2 teaspoons kosher salt

¼ cup olive oil
Cornmeal or wheat bran for dusting
  (optional)
Toppings (see below)

In a large plastic container (16 by 11 by 4 inches works well) with a lid, combine the water, yeast, flour, salt, and olive oil. Use your hands to combine the mixture. You do not need to knead the dough; just combine all the ingredients so there are no dry spots and everything is incorporated. It will look ROUGH, and that's okay. As you move through the resting/folding process, it will begin to resemble a real dough.

Place the lid on the container and let the dough rest for 30 minutes at room temperature.

After the rest, stretch and fold all four sides of the dough into the center, allowing them to overlap as if you were wrapping a present (see page xviii). Flip the dough over so the sides do not unravel. Let the dough rest for another 30 minutes, giving it time to relax. While you are waiting, you can spread olive oil on the bottom and edges of a sheet pan if you plan to make a thick-crust pie.

continued

Turn the dough out on a lightly floured surface. Divide the dough into two equal pieces and round slightly for individual pies. Or leave it whole and press it into a sheet pan for a "Grandma-style" or focaccia-style pie.

At this point, the dough can be baked immediately or covered and refrigerated overnight to create a thinner, more flavorful crust. (The protein in the flour denatures overnight as the dough ferments, which makes it easier to stretch into a thin sheet of pizza dough.)

When ready to bake, preheat the oven to 425°F. Carefully stretch your dough balls into 10 to 12-inch rounds using your hands. If you try to roll them with a rolling pin, you will be cursing me for days—the dough doesn't like that so much. Stretching with your hands is much easier. Dredge one side of each piece of dough in cornmeal or wheat bran. This will be the bottom of your pizza and prevent it from sticking to your pan. It also adds a nice texture.

Press your fingertips into the dough to create dimples in the surface. This will break up any giant air bubbles. The dough should expand as you are "dimpling" it. You can also gently stretch it to create a thinner crust. Brush the dough with olive oil and add desired toppings. Bake for 20 minutes, until golden brown on the bottom. Pizza will keep wrapped airtight in the fridge for up to 2 days, but it is best eaten immediately.

Toppings (the amounts listed are enough for two pizzas; add the toppings before baking, unless noted otherwise):

TOMATO BASIL: Spread ½ cup canned crushed tomatoes over each pizza crust, all the way to the edges. Top each pizza with 4 ounces cubed fresh mozzarella and bake. Top each baked pizza with five or six fresh basil leaves.

FIG-PROSCIUTTO: Spread 2 tablespoons fig jam over each pizza crust. Top each pizza with 8 slices prosciutto and 4 ounces goat cheese. After baking, top each pizza with 1 cup baby arugula and drizzle with ½ tablespoon balsamic vinegar.

SPICY SAUSAGE: Cook 4 links of hot Italian sausage in a sauté pan, breaking the meat apart into crumbles. Drain the grease. Spread ½ cup canned crushed tomatoes over each pizza crust, all the way to the edges. Sprinkle the sausage crumbles over the sauce, dividing evenly. Sprinkle ½ cup of assorted sliced peppers (hot or sweet), followed by 4 ounces of cubed mozarella over each pizza.

BURRATA-PESTO: Spread ¼ cup basil pesto evenly across each pizza crust. Scatter ½ pint of halved cherry tomatoes over the pesto on each pizza. Finish each pizza with 4 ounces of burrata, pulled apart in chunks.

RICOTTA, CORN, ASPARAGUS & FONTINA: Cut kernels off of 1 ear of corn. Cut 1 bunch asparagus into ¼-inch pieces. Spread ¼ cup ricotta cheese evenly across each pizza crust. Top with corn, asparagus, and 1 cup grated fontina cheese.

OLIVE-CAPER-ANCHOVY: Spread ½ cup canned crushed tomatoes over each pizza crust. Spread ¼ cup drained kalamata olives, 2 tablespoons drained capers, ½ tin anchovies, and 4 ounces of cubed fresh mozzarella across each pizza.

YANA'S MOM'S GRANOLA

Makes 15 cups (see note)

After my disastrous bike crash, my first few days in the hospital were rough. Meal deliveries were inconsistent, sometimes nonexistent, and altogether inedible. Yana, who was with me during my accident, brought me a fresh batch of granola her mom made and shipped from California. She told me that as a teenager, it was the only thing she could be convinced to eat. It sustained me for the rest of my stay. Yana renewed my supply when I was released. It continued to be my go-to recovery food, then turned into fuel for my workouts as physical therapy progressed. Then Yana's mom's oven broke, and the granola supply dried up. She sent us her recipe so we could make our own. Now it's flying off the shelves at Montclair Bread Company. This granola is wholesome: not too sweet, and rich in nutrients. Its simplicity makes it easy on the stomach. Yana's mom gave us her blessing to make this recipe our own. You can substitute different nuts or dried fruits. I make mine exactly as she made hers because it's perfect the way it is.

NOTE: This recipe makes a lot of granola, but it keeps for 4 to 6 weeks if you store it in an airtight container. I prefer to make a big batch that will stick around for a while rather than a smaller batch that will only get me through next week. I store my granola in gallon-size resealable plastic bags or, if I'm feeling fancy, mason jars!

1 cup olive oil

½ cup honey

1 teaspoon vanilla extract

10 cups rolled oats

¾ cup raw cashews, divided

¾ cup raw sliced almonds, divided

¾ cup walnut halves and pieces, divided

¾ cup sunflower seeds, divided

1 cup sweetened shredded coconut

1 cup raisins

Preheat the oven to 325°F.

In a large pot over low heat, warm the oil, honey, and vanilla, stirring until blended.

Remove from the heat and stir in the oats until evenly coated.

Add half the cashews, almonds, walnuts, and sunflower seeds, setting aside the remaining half.

Spread the oat mixture in a single layer on a baking sheet.

Bake for 1 hour, stirring every 20 minutes so the ingredients are evenly toasted.

Remove from the oven. Pour the granola into a large mixing bowl and toss with the remaining untoasted nuts and seeds, as well as the coconut and raisins. Let the granola cool and store in an airtight container at room temperature.

GRAIN SALADS

Makes 4 servings

Every summer, I travel to Skowhegan, Maine, to attend the Kneading Conference hosted by the Maine Grain Alliance. Their mission is to inspire and empower people who are building local grain economies, such as farmers, millers, bakers, and chefs. Through the years, I have been able to sample heirloom varieties of grains grown in the Northeast: farro, oats, quinoa, kamut, sirvinta, red fife, and warthog wheat. In addition to baking with the grains, I started using them in salads. These became a staple at the bakery in the summertime. Grains in their whole form are packed with nutrients, making these salads a super healthy summer meal. Not only can I highlight the grain but also it allows me to use fresh, seasonal veggies from my local farmers.

1 cup dried grains (such as wheat berries, farro, or quinoa)

1½ cups water

2 cups chopped vegetables (such as cherry tomatoes, asparagus, peppers, cucumbers, zucchini, or corn), cut into bite-sized pieces

½ cup olive oil

¼ cup rice vinegar

1 tablespoon soy sauce

1 teaspoon sesame oil

1 teaspoon honey

Place the grains and water in a small pot over medium-high heat; bring to a boil. Decrease the heat to low, cover, and simmer for about 20 minutes, or until the grains are soft and plump and have absorbed all the water. Spread the grains onto a baking sheet in a thin layer; refrigerate until cool, about 20 minutes.

While you're waiting, chop the veggies. In a small bowl, stir together the olive oil, rice vinegar, soy sauce, sesame oil, and honey. When the grains are cool, spoon them into a large bowl with the veggies. Pour the dressing over and toss to combine. The grain salad can be served as is or over a bed of greens. It will keep wrapped airtight in the fridge for up to 5 days.

OVERNIGHT OATS

If you need a quick, on-the-go breakfast you can set up the night before, this is it. My alarm is set fifteen minutes before I have to walk out the door to go to the bakery in the morning. Breakfast is the last thing on my mind. Having these oats ready to go makes the most difficult task remembering to grab them from the fridge before I leave the house.

1 cup rolled oats (quick oats will work but may be mushier)
1 cup milk of your choice

Optional mix-ins
1 tablespoon chia seeds
¼ cup shredded unsweetened coconut
1 tablespoon nut or sunflower butter
1 tablespoon maple syrup, honey, or agave

Optional toppings
Fresh berries
Nuts
Dried fruit

Stir the oats and milk together, along with any additions, if desired, and refrigerate for at least 8 hours before it is ready to eat. I love to make mine in mason jars because the screwtop lids allow me to grab a jar on the go if I'm running out the door in the morning. Add toppings, if desired, when ready to eat. Oats will keep wrapped airtight in the fridge for up to 3 days.

ENERGY BARS

For years I tried to find a recipe for a "granola bar" that had a soft, almost chewy consistency, but I kept striking out with crunchy or cakey bars. When I started making chia pudding, I realized that the chia could be a helpful binder in a bar recipe. Combined with the flax and the oats, it all comes together. These are a great not-too-sweet, on-the-go grab to get a quick energy boost. Also, my kids LOVE them. Please don't tell them there's healthy stuff in the mix.

½ cup chia seeds

½ cup whole flaxseeds

2 cups rolled oats

1 cup unsweetened shredded coconut

1 cup coconut water

1¼ cups peanut butter or almond butter

2 cups almond flour or ground almonds

1 cup mini chocolate chips (or substitute regular)

½ cup honey

In a large bowl, mix together the chia seeds, flaxseeds, oats, coconut, and coconut water. Cover tightly with plastic wrap and refrigerate for at least 4 hours, or overnight, to allow the mixture to absorb the liquid.

Add the peanut butter, almond flour, chocolate chips, and honey; mix well. It should have the consistency of Play-Doh.

Grease a 9 by 13-inch sheet pan and press in the mixture or roll into tablespoon-sized balls. Refrigerate for 2 hours until firm. If using a sheet pan, cut the mixture into 2-inch bars. These will keep wrapped airtight in the fridge for up to 2 weeks.

CHOCOLATE-PEANUT BUTTER ENERGY BITES

Makes 16 bites

My kids are sugar fiends. They can locate sweets anywhere, anytime. In an effort to curb the excess, I discovered they love these energy bites. I made them for myself to serve as an afternoon pick-me-up, but soon I was doubling the recipe to make enough for the whole family.

These are gluten-free if you use certified gluten-free oats.

1 cup quick oats or rolled oats, pulsed a few times in a food processor
½ cup ground flaxseed
3 tablespoons cocoa powder
¼ teaspoon sea salt

½ cup peanut butter or other nut butter
⅓ cup maple syrup or honey
1 teaspoon vanilla extract (optional)
1 tablespoon unsweetened almond milk or milk of your choice

In a large mixing bowl, combine the oats, flaxseed, cocoa powder, sea salt, peanut butter, and maple syrup. If the dough is too thick and sticky, add a little almond milk.

Roll the dough into 1-inch balls. They can be placed in an airtight container or sandwich bag. Chill in the refrigerator for at least 20 minutes before serving. These will keep wrapped airtight in the fridge for up to 7 days or in the freezer for up to 1 month.

STEEL-CUT OATMEAL

Makes 4 to 6 servings

I took Montclair Bread's leadership team to the Hudson Valley for an overnight retreat. We visited my dear friend and mentor, Sharon Burns-Leader, at Bread Alone Bakery in Kingston, New York, which I believe sets the standard for quality in baking, service, and atmosphere.

While we were there, I had a bowl of steel-cut oatmeal that blew my mind. I could have reached out to Sharon to ask for her recipe, but I didn't (I did tell her how much I adored every bite). I thought it would be easy to figure out because I'd worked with oats in every way imaginable over the years. Nope—not easy. I very quickly became OBSESSED with perfecting the texture of my oats.

At the risk of embarrassing myself . . . I still don't know Sharon's secrets, but here's the two-day technique that has been working well for me. NOTE: this recipe is specifically for steel-cut oats. Rolled or instant would be a completely different ballgame.

1 cup steel-cut oats

2 cups water

4 cups milk of your choice, divided

Maple syrup, nut butter, or fresh fruit, to top (optional)

Preheat the oven to 350°F.

Spread the oats onto an ungreased baking sheet and toast for 8 to 10 minutes, until just starting to brown and you can smell the toasty oats.

While the oats are toasting, heat the water in a medium pot over medium-high heat, bring it to a rapid boil, and then remove it from the heat. When the oats are toasted and still hot, put them into the hot water. Cover them with a lid and leave them at room temperature overnight.

On day 2, place the oats over medium-low heat, pour in 2 cups of the milk, then stir and bring and bring to a simmer. Cook for 30 minutes, stirring every 5 to 10 minutes. Add the remaining 2 cups milk and simmer for another 60 to 90 minutes, stirring every 5 to 10 minutes, until the oats have absorbed all of the milk. The oats will go from dense and brown to fluffy and white as they start to burst open.

Serve topped with maple syrup, nut butter, or fresh fruit, if desired.

Oatmeal will keep wrapped airtight in the fridge for up to 5 days. When you reheat it, you may want to add more milk, as it will thicken when cold.

BUTTERMILK BISCUITS

Makes 8 to 10 biscuits

You really can't go wrong with a tender, buttery buttermilk biscuit. They make the perfect addition to any stew. Use them to make a Southern-style sausage and egg sandwich for breakfast or fill them with strawberries and whipped cream for a shortcake dessert.

2½ cups all-purpose flour

2 tablespoons sugar

4 teaspoons baking powder

1 teaspoon kosher salt

½ cup (1 stick) cold unsalted butter, cut into ¼-inch cubes

1 large egg

¾ cup (6 ounces) buttermilk

Preheat the oven to 375°F.

Place the flour, sugar, baking powder, and salt in a large bowl and stir together. Toss the butter cubes into the flour mixture and squish the butter between your fingers to flatten it into flakes.

In a separate small bowl, whisk the egg into the buttermilk.

Make a well in the center of the flour mixture and pour the egg mixture into the well. Use your hands to bring all the ingredients together; squeeze and turn the mass until it becomes a ball of dough. Try your best to keep the butter chunks intact: that's what makes for flaky biscuits.

Pull off tennis-ball-sized pieces of dough and place the lumps about 2 inches apart on a baking sheet. Brush with buttermilk and bake for 15 to 20 minutes, until lightly browned on top. Biscuits will keep wrapped airtight at room temperature for up to 3 days.

FRUIT COBBLER

Preheat the oven to 375°F. In a 9 by 13-inch baking pan, toss 8 cups fresh or frozen berries with ½ cup sugar and 1 tablespoon cornstarch. Proceed with the biscuit recipe, but pull off raw dough lumps about the size of golf balls and arrange them in an even layer over the berries. Bake until the berries are bubbly and the biscuits are brown, about 20 minutes.

COCONUT CAKE

This is one of my grandfather's favorites. Mombo always made coconut cake for Easter, Christmas, and occasionally just because. I later learned that the first coconut cakes in America were made by enslaved people in the South who had brought from Africa the knowledge of how to break down a coconut. Coconut cakes continued to be linked to Southern black culture. In the 1950s they were sold by the Club from Nowhere, a collective of black bakers led by Georgia Gilmore, who organized the group after being fired from her cafeteria job because of her involvement in the civil rights movement. The women used the proceeds from their coconut cake sales to pay for gasoline and alternative transportation, making the Montgomery Bus Boycotts possible. In 2020, in order to be better allies in the fight against racism, we honored the coconut cake in a community bake-along and fundraiser for the National Coalition of 100 Black Women, eventually raising over $4,000.

Cake

3¼ cups all-purpose flour
2 cups granulated sugar
2½ teaspoons baking powder
1 teaspoon kosher salt
¾ cup (1½ sticks) unsalted butter, melted
1¼ cups canned coconut milk
4 large eggs

Frosting

1 cup (2 sticks) unsalted butter, at room temperature
3½ cups (1 pound) confectioners' sugar
¼ cup coconut milk

1 (7-ounce) bag sweetened shredded coconut

Preheat the oven to 350°F. Grease two 8-inch cake pans with melted butter and dust with flour.

To make the cake, stir together the flour, sugar, baking powder, and salt in a large bowl. Add the melted butter; stir until the mixture looks pebble-y.

In a medium bowl, whisk the coconut milk and eggs together. Add a third of the milk mixture to the dry ingredients; stir until pasty. Repeat two more times with a third of the liquid mixture. This process helps avoid lumps in the batter.

continued

Divide the batter between the pans. Bake the cakes for about 25 minutes, or until a toothpick inserted in the center comes out clean. Remove the cakes from the pans while they are still hot and let cool on a rack.

While the cakes cool, make your frosting. In the bowl of a stand mixer fitted with a paddle attachment, cream the butter on medium-high speed. When it's white and fluffy, add the confectioners' sugar and mix on low to medium speed to incorporate. Add the coconut milk and mix to incorporate, then whip on medium-high speed for 3 to 4 minutes. It should be fluffy and easy to spread with a spatula.

To assemble the cake, use a long serrated knife to shave the dome off each cooled cake layer. Using a spatula, spread an even coating of frosting on the top of a layer and sprinkle with coconut. Smear some frosting on the bottom of the remaining layer, then stack on top. Cover the assembled cake with frosting and sprinkle with coconut. The cake is best served at room temperature, but it can be carefully wrapped with plastic wrap against the cut side and stored at room temperature for up to 4 days.

Montclair Burrito Co.

My favorite part of owning a small business is the ability to make decisions quickly. I don't need to sit around a boardroom table and discuss options. I don't need to sign off from multiple levels across multiple departments. I just take a leap of faith.

In early 2019, the Montclair Bread Co. team realized April 1 would fall on a Monday, typically the slowest sales day of the week. We started kicking around some ideas for April Fool's Day doughnuts, and someone suggested we turn the whole bakery into a taco shop for the day. Before I could stop the momentum, my bakery manager, Jessie, designed a new logo, and we dreamed up a menu. Then I thought, since we're already MBCo, we should make burritos instead of tacos.

I'm notoriously bad at keeping secrets, but I managed to keep my mouth shut for two months, despite my excitement! During that time, we went all in—we printed customized staff shirts, signs, and stickers. As the big day approached, the bakery began to smell like a Mexican grandma's house. On Sunday night, I posted the following message on Instagram and Facebook.

"It has been almost seven years since I launched Montclair Bread Company . . . I've worked around the clock to bake the best artisan breads and doughnuts, often starting in the early hours of the morning to make sure everything is ready in time for the doors to open at 6 a.m.

"After much consideration and longing to have more sleep and balance in my life, I've decided to leave the Montclair Bread Company behind. Today, I am relaunching this business and am happy to announce the opening of the Montclair Burrito Company!!"

I was shocked by how angry so many people were when they read the news and feared the loss of our doughnuts. But the first customer in the door asked how she could get her own Montclair Burrito Co. shirt. We were off to the races!

And the burritos—made from carnitas roasted in the oven, of course—were a hit.

CHAPTER

05

RECIPES FROM QUARANTINE

By March 2020, I had a team of thirty-two bakers and retail employees. Our sales were as strong as ever. My family had never been happier. I was hitting paces I never thought I could in my training runs, with several races coming up on my calendar. I was finally feeling a sense of stability.

Then the coronavirus pandemic hit.

Within days, I had laid off more than half my staff, and I was desperately trying to keep my business open, my family healthy, and my community fed.

March 15 (Day 1): I spent all day calling people and telling them they were being laid off. I had no idea how long I would be able to keep the bakery open. With every new day came a new executive order from New Jersey Governor Phil Murphy, forcing more businesses to close. I thought it was just a matter of time before mine was next. Though the bakery had a strong first quarter, I wouldn't be able to make payments on all of our debts; continue to pay my vendors, my landlord, and the electric company; *and* keep a roof over my own head without some kind of daily income. I knew I had to figure out how to work within the boundaries and sell whatever I could, however I could, to stay afloat.

March 20 (Day 6): For the first time in the history of Montclair Bread Co., everyone forgot about the doughnuts. All they wanted was bread. So I baked as much sandwich bread as I could, using the only sixteen loaf pans I owned. I was afraid to spend money to purchase more pans. I had also worked three twenty-hour days in a row, doing the work of the twenty people I had laid off.

My friends and social media followers told me they couldn't find bread at the grocery store. Flour and yeast were also wiped out everywhere, and fresh fruit, veggies, sugar, eggs, milk, oats, and bacon were in short supply.

Well, our usual restaurant suppliers had all of that. So that became our menu. Every item sold out immediately. I had no idea how long our suppliers would have these items.

Whenever they too reported they were out of stock, I bounced to another company. I ordered from as many different places as I could.

I was terrified and full of anxiety, but I just kept putting one foot in front of the other. I focused only on making it through each day.

I ordered forty more loaf pans.

March 24 (Day 10): I started baking at 2 a.m. My team and I worked out a plan to set up our patio with pickup orders arranged on tables lined up and filled with orders organized alphabetically.

We were baking more than our ovens could handle, and it still wasn't enough. Everything we posted for sale online was snatched up within minutes.

I went for a run to try to clear my head. When I returned, I found a patio packed with customers standing much, much closer together than the safe six-feet-apart guidelines. It looked like prepandemic pizza party times. First, I panicked. Then I began drawing lines in chalk on the sidewalk, six feet apart. And I started looking for a bouncer.

April 10 (Day 27): I wrote to customers:

Find a way to say yes. That's part of our credo. Only now, in this new normal, I feel like all we've been saying is "no." No, I can't make a doughnut cake for your husband's birthday this year. No, you're not allowed to come inside and buy a baguette today. No, I'm not able to sell you one single doughnut. No, I don't have the resources to make your favorite flavor this month even though it's always on our menu. No, the items you ordered for yesterday or tomorrow are not available for you to pick up today.

Every single doughnut, every single loaf of bread is promised to someone before we start baking it each day. We take great care and consideration in making yours special. We are producing to the peak of our ability, which means we don't have any extras.

The other part of our credo that I have to fall back on when you tell me that I'm running a terrible business because you can't have what you want because I simply don't have it to give . . . when you scream at my staff and threaten to write a negative Yelp review (yes, really) because you mistakenly ordered for the wrong day . . . the other part of our credo states . . . "we are real passionate people, with all the strengths and weaknesses real people have. We are your neighbors. Together, we build community."

Trust me when I say, I have felt, really deeply felt, every weakness within myself and my business this week. I have pushed to the limits of time, physical strength, and mental capacity as has every single person on my team and for what? To feed you! To nourish you! Because I value each and every one of you and I want to make a small part of this ordeal better for everyone, the only way I know how—through food. I'm scared too. I'm terrified. I don't want anyone in my family or on my staff to get sick. I'm taking every precaution I can to continue doing what I love, while staying healthy and keeping everyone around me healthy.

Please remember that we are your neighbors and we are real people and we have real limits. None of us had a plan for these circumstances. We don't know what we're doing! If it looks like we do, it's because we have a really good game face.

April 13 (Day 30, right after Easter): I wrote to customers:

We did it! We made it through the holidays in quarantine. Thank you for all of your messages, especially the handwritten note left in the trunk of a car during curbside pick-up. Wow! I knew I loved this community, but the outpouring of kindness and gratitude my staff and I received over the weekend was tremendous.

From the time I decided to make a career in baking, I chose bread. When I developed the initial business plan for my bakery, it was inspired by the pictures of NYC bread lines during the Depression. I was actually going to name the bakery "The Bread Line."

For the first time in the life of Montclair Bread Co, since the doughnuts became the shining stars six months after I opened, bread sales are rising (pun intended!). This makes my baker heart so freaking happy. Don't get me wrong, I adore the doughnuts, but baking bread warms my soul in a way I can't begin to describe—especially when I know the loaves have a home to go to.

April 17 (Day 34): I wrote to customers:

These things, these tough times, we learn from them, even if it doesn't seem like it while we're suffering. Trying to maintain some semblance of normalcy—"working" from home, entertaining a house full of kids, preparing every meal yourself, waiting for hours for an

Instacart slot to open . . . you will learn from this. You will be more resilient. You will know that whatever comes after this, will be easy because you've already been through hell and back.

April 18 (Day 35): I wrote an FAQ for customers:

Are you selling sourdough starter?

Nope, we only make what we need to leaven our breads, but you can make your own in just 5 days using the flour you purchased from us. It's way more fun to feed your own.

I tried baking something new at home and it didn't come out as planned, can you help?

Yes!!! I (Rachel) can try. Email me your questions, pictures help, and I'll do my best to get back to you. You can follow my personal instagram feed @rachelrwyman for the recipes I've been baking during quarantine.

When will this be over???

Not soon enough.

April 20 (Day 37): I wrote to customers:

I am hosting a #MBCBakeAlong. As most of you know, I've been posting a recipe each day on my personal instagram account. Today, I launched a contest to get you even more excited about baking MBCo signature items at home. Each week, I will post a different Bake Along recipe. This week's recipe is for Cinnamon Buns [page 94]! Absolute worst case scenario—you'll have a tray of cinnamon buns for participating.

April 24 (Day 40): I wrote to customers:

This week, we lost another piece of equipment—our retail refrigerator decided it could not go on one more day filled with eggs, milk, and butter. I had no choice. I spent money I don't have to spend and replaced it so we can continue to stock these items. The new fridge arrived yesterday bolted onto a pallet, dropped into the center of our bakery. And there it sat. Six of us stood staring, trying to figure out what we were going to do. We didn't have anyone to call and we certainly didn't have the forklift recommended in the instruction manual.

It was after 2 p.m., the entire staff was leaving to go home. But they didn't. I watched as a photographer, an actor, a costume designer, a customer service manager, and a retail manager came up with a strategy and ultimately lifted the 1000 lbs of cooling glory off the pallet and into its new home. It was kind of like that time I was subjected to that team building task at summer camp where you had to find a way to pass everyone through a spiderweb of ropes without using the same hole twice, only the stakes were much higher. I also feel like we're on a new season of the "Real World," or maybe it's "Survivor," and I'm just waiting for the producer to show up and tell us it's over—we've done enough.

This has been a pretty heavy week to be a small business owner. I was interviewed for a Bloomberg story about Shake Shack's $10 million loan. I voiced my opinion about the *government funding that is supposed to be available to help businesses like mine. Shortly after this was posted, I received a call from Danny Meyer to thank me for my kindness in the story [toward Shake Shack employees]. I've admired him and his business practices since I baked the seeded rolls he served at Union Square Cafe and the semolina raisin fennel breads for Gramercy Tavern while working overnight at Amy's Bread. He told me he was honored to be mentioned alongside me, but the honor is truly all mine.*

As we continue to support our community, I urge you to think with kindness and compassion. Point your anger in the right direction. Big or small (and that's just perspective), there are good people being forced to make very difficult decisions, all in an attempt to provide for as many families as possible. The guy flipping your burgers on the line at Shake Shack isn't any less deserving of a paycheck than the guy shaping your baguettes at Montclair Bread Co.

April 27 (Day 43): I wrote to customers:

We are in this together.

And this week, we ate a lot of cinnamon buns together! I am so impressed, not elementary-school-art-show impressed, but really impressed, by all of your buns. Some of you used yeast for the very first time and you did it so well. Some of you shared the project with your

kids—LOVED the sprinkles, pink frosting and chocolate additions. Some of you taunted your pups with the buns . . . I hope they got their treats too. ALL of you made me love this community so much more. Thank you for accepting this challenge with wide open arms.

Next up: Homemade Pop Tarts [page 30]

May 7 (Day 53): I wrote to customers:

Sunday is Mother's Day! I hope you can take a minute to recognize how much you've accomplished this year. The world has put you in an impossible position, yet you are still surviving. I haven't folded laundry in six weeks. It's in a pile on my sofa that eventually falls on the floor and gets washed again before regaining its position at the top of the pile . . . If that doesn't help you feel better about everything you're accomplishing in quarantine, I don't know what will!

May 11 (Day 57): I wrote to customers:

#MBCbakealong is still going strong. How cool is it that we're all doing the same thing & enjoying the same dessert—it's almost like we're all together—right?!?!

It gets harder and harder to pick a winner from all the absolutely incredible entries we receive. Again, I'm so sorry I can't gift you all with a prize but I promise you'll all be invited to my big post-quarantine party!!! You can bring me desserts, okay?

May 15 (Day 61): I wrote to customers:

Last night could not have been more perfect. It was the first time I've felt some semblance of "real" life in the last two months. Brad got a fire going in my outdoor oven, I baked pizzas on the bakery patio and we dined alfresco with the kids. Well, I ate standing up by the oven and they got up from the table every two minutes to chase each other around the building but we almost enjoyed a meal together.

Still, after savoring every second of the evening, I felt sad and empty. It was a glaring reminder of what my business has lost, what all of our businesses have lost.

Yes, Montclair Bread Co, is surviving in quarantine. We sell out of most items daily. There is a line of people to pick up their orders. From the outside, it looks like we are thriving.

Here's the thing and this is important . . . we are making the most with what we have. We are selling out because what we're able to produce with our staff of ten is far less than we were able to with our team of 30+. I can't rehire people because we don't have the space to safely work with more bodies. We have canceled all three weeks of summer baking camp. There will not be pizza nights with live music and a packed patio for the foreseeable future. Even if there were large orders for weddings, birthdays and graduations (which there aren't) we couldn't fill them. The baking classes I teach, which pay my salary, are postponed indefinitely. Our new offerings exclude made-to-order breakfast sandwiches and drip coffee which made up 50 percent of our normal daily sales.

Yes, Montclair Bread Co is surviving in quarantine. The business we are currently operating is sustaining us. We can keep going for one more day. We can pay our staff, we can pay our rent and for that I am truly grateful.

I wanted to reach out to provide a look behind the scenes of my business because I hope it helps you make decisions in how you support ALL of our local small businesses. Sure, your favorite restaurant may have filled up their delivery capacity, you favorite bike shop might not have any appointments left to accommodate your tune up, your favorite hardware store might be sold out of trash bags . . . it doesn't mean "they're killing it" in quarantine, it means they can exist for one more day and hopefully, they will exist when we make it to the other side of this. No one is killing it in quarantine.

June 1 (Day 78): I wrote to customers:

I've been thinking a lot about the Once-ler from Dr. Seuss's book, the Lorax. I don't make "thneeds," but I can relate to his growth trajectory, his need to make his operation bigger. For the last eight years, I've been biggering . . . jumping on every opportunity to expand my

business . . . making more and more and more doughnuts as the lines get longer. It hasn't been about trying to make more money, it's been out of fear. If the person at the end of the line doesn't get a doughnut, they might not come back.

Running a business during quarantine has forced me to look at what matters most, to strip everything back to the bare essentials and rebuild. I've learned so much in a very short time. I don't want to be the Once-ler anymore. The biggering is coming to an end.

July 13 (Day 120): I wrote to customers:

I am a mom of three children who are enrolled in the Montclair Public Schools. I am an essential worker. I cannot "virtually" bake bread and make doughnuts (but wouldn't that be cool?!). In order to support my family and keep my business going, I have to leave home to work each day. I am part *of an incredible team of bakers and retail employees who are also essential to this operation and who leave their families to come to work each day. I live, work and play in Montclair. I am your neighbor.*

I have all of the fears and anxieties you do. I worry about the health and safety of my family and of my staff. I worry about the state of my children's education and who will be there to help them learn in the fall while I work outside of my home. I worry about the future of my bakery. Will it outlast this crisis?

August 1 (Day 139): I wrote to customers:

I face an uncertain future by focusing on the mile that I am in. I get through today. I remember why I started this business in the first place: because I love the people. I love that the woman who came in every morning for coffee back when the bakery was always empty was eventually joined by a man, and then they served my doughnuts at their wedding reception. They still come in with their two children, and I saw them in line during the quarantine, masks on.

In some ways, I live for the stress of running this bakery. I love that in a pinch, I have figured out how to make doughnuts without a mixer or without milk. If I didn't know what it was like to pivot on a dime and come up with plans B, C and D, maybe I would still be using a cane to walk down the stairs instead of racing 5Ks. Maybe I'd be bowled over with anxiety over the state of the world, instead of just trying to make my corner of the universe a little better.

In the end, I am grateful for this life, this path I have been given.

BASIC WHITE BREAD

Makes 2 loaves

Everyone became a baker in quarantine. After seeing one too many photos of failed bread attempts, and after receiving a slew of recipe requests, I shared my favorite basic white bread on Instagram. It's a simple, no-frills, all-purpose white sandwich loaf. You don't need to create a starter dough a day in advance. The dough can be mixed by hand, and the loaves come together quickly. This is the best starting point for anyone wanting to dip their toe into the world of magic, creating food with gluten and yeast.

4¼ cups all-purpose flour
1 teaspoon sugar
1½ teaspoons instant yeast

½ teaspoon kosher salt
1¾ cups water, at room temperature
1 tablespoon vegetable oil

In a large mixing bowl, stir together the flour, sugar, yeast, and salt. Add the water and oil and work the dough into a compact ball. No need to knead; just gather all the ingredients until they are incorporated. Cover the bowl with plastic wrap or an unscented kitchen-sized garbage bag and let rest for about 1 hour, or until the dough has started to rise and forms a dome in the center.

Fold all four sides of the dough into the center, allowing them to overlap as if you were wrapping a present (see page xviii). Flip the dough over so the sides do not unravel. Re-cover with plastic wrap and let rest for another hour, until you see the dough start to form a dome in the center.

Grease two loaf pans using vegetable oil. Scrape the dough onto a floured work surface. Divide it into two equal pieces. Pat one piece into a 4 by 6-inch rectangle. Pick up one of the shorter ends and fold the dough to the middle of the rectangle. Press the dough in with your fingertips, working with as little flour as possible, so that the dough adheres to itself. (You are creating tension along the surface.) Fold the dough again so it meets the other short end, and use the heel of your hand to press down, sealing it up. Give the dough a little shake to even it out and place it, seam side down, into a greased loaf pan. Repeat with the other piece of dough. Cover the loaves loosely with plastic wrap and let them rise for about 2 hours or until they start to crest above the top of the loaf pan.

Preheat the oven to 400°F. Uncover the loaves. Brush or spray them with water and use a serrated knife to cut a long slash down the center of each loaf.

Bake for 20 to 25 minutes, until the top is brown and the loaves sound hollow when tapped. Once they are finished baking, remove the loaves from the pans immediately by carefully tapping the side of the pan. If the bread is sticking, you may need to run a paring knife along the edge of the pan to release the loaf. Lay the loaves on their sides on your table to allow air to circulate around them as they cool. If you allow the bread to cool in the pans, condensation builds up around the bottom and edges, and the loaves will be soggy. Loaves will keep wrapped lightly in a tea towel at room temperature for 24 to 48 hours maximum. They are best eaten fresh. (Wrapping them in plastic wrap will soften the crust.) They can be wrapped airtight and frozen for several months.

CHEESE CRACKERS

Makes about 60 bite-sized crackers

About three weeks into quarantine, I became tired of the nonstop whining about not having any "salty snacks" in the house and convinced the kids to help me make cheese crackers. I think the actual request was for Goldfish. If your inner Pinterest mom wants to find mini cookie cutters and make fun shapes out of the dough, go for it. I do not play that game. We went for the Cheese Nips look, way less effort. I used cheddar and swiss, but feel free to play around with whatever cheese you have in the house.

¼ cup (½ stick) unsalted butter, at room temperature

8 ounces grated cheese (about 2 cups)

1 teaspoon kosher salt

1 cup all-purpose flour

3 tablespoons cold water

Optional spices (pick one; I'm not suggesting all of them at the same time, but hey, they're your crackers . . .)

¼ teaspoon ground cayenne pepper

1 tablespoon fresh chopped herbs

1 teaspoon ground black pepper

1 teaspoon dried red pepper flakes

In the bowl of a stand mixer fitted with a paddle attachment, cream together the butter, cheese, and salt on medium-high speed until it is smooth. (You can also use a food processor or stir by hand.) Add the flour and mix on low speed until the dough looks like sandy pebbles. Add the water and spice or herbs, if using, and mix until a dough ball forms. Remove the dough from the mixer and pat it into a 4-inch square, wrap it tightly in plastic wrap, and refrigerate it for at least 30 minutes.

Preheat the oven to 350°F. On a floured work surface, roll the dough into a rectangle about ¼ inch thick. Using a straight edge and a pizza cutter, cut the dough into 1-inch strips, then cut in the other direction to make squares.

Line a baking sheet with parchment paper, and evenly space the squares on the sheet. Poke holes in the center with a fork to vent the steam during baking. Bake for 8 to 10 minutes, until the crackers reach your desired level of color and crisp.

Crackers will keep wrapped airtight at room temperature for up to 2 weeks. I promise they won't be around that long.

FLOUR TORTILLAS

We ate rice bowls for breakfast, lunch, and dinner for the first three weeks of the pandemic. Then we started craving tacos. But we didn't have tortillas, and I was unwilling to venture out to the grocery store, so I decided to make my own. It's not a time-consuming process. The whole ordeal takes less than an hour, including resting time.

2½ cups all-purpose flour
1 teaspoon baking powder
½ teaspoon kosher salt

⅞ cup water (this is a weird number, I know, but ¾ isn't enough, and 1 cup is too much, so . . .)
¼ cup vegetable oil

In a large bowl, stir together the flour, baking powder, and salt. Make a well in the center and pour the water and oil into the well. Pull the flour from the side into the well and mix until you can form a ball of dough. You can knead it a little until it comes together. Cover the dough with plastic wrap and let it rest for 30 minutes.

On a floured work surface, divide your dough into eight equal pieces. Using a floured rolling pin, roll each piece into an 8-inch circle. (If you'd like smaller tortillas, cut the dough into more pieces.) If the dough fights back, roll it halfway, let it rest for a couple minutes, and give it another go—this allows the gluten some time to relax. Repeat with the remaining pieces of dough. Cover the dough with plastic wrap or an unscented kitchen-sized garbage bag so it doesn't dry out while you continue working.

Heat a dry frying pan or griddle over medium heat (you don't want it too hot or the tortillas will burn before they cook through).

Place a dough circle on the pan and cook for 30 to 60 seconds on each side. Flip when the cooked side just starts to brown. Transfer the cooked tortillas to a plate and immediately cover with a kitchen towel. This will keep them from drying out until you finish cooking the rest. Tortillas are best eaten fresh. I would not recommend storing them for later use.

BAGELS

During the pandemic, a lot of our local bagel shops closed and these breakfast staples became difficult to find. Many customers reached out to ask whether I would make them. Instead of turning Montclair Bread into a bagel shop, I shared my favorite bagel recipe. I watched with pride as my social media feeds lit up with pictures of everyone's home-baked creations.

5 cups all-purpose or bread flour, plus additional for dusting

2 teaspoons kosher salt

1½ teaspoons instant yeast

8 to 10 cups water, divided

1 teaspoon plus 1 tablespoon molasses or dark corn syrup or maple syrup, divided

Optional toppings of your choice (such as sesame seeds, poppy seeds, Spicy Everything Mix, recipe follows)

Day 1: In the bowl of a stand mixer fitted with a dough hook, combine the flour, salt, yeast, 2 cups of the water, and 1 teaspoon of the molasses. Mix on low until the ingredients come together, then increase to medium speed and mix the dough for 10 to 12 minutes. The dough will look dry, almost like you forgot something, but it comes together into a smooth, tight lump. Cover the dough ball with plastic wrap or place it in an airtight container and let it rest for 30 minutes.

Flour a sheet pan. Turn the dough out onto a lightly floured surface. Divide the dough into 12 equal pieces. Roll each piece into a 6-inch rope. Be careful not to roll it too long or you will have skinny bagels. Wrap the rope around the back of your hand with the ends in your palm. Place your palm on the table and roll back and forth twice to seal the ends. You should have something resembling a bagel. Place your bagels onto the sheet pan and cover with plastic wrap. Refrigerate them overnight.

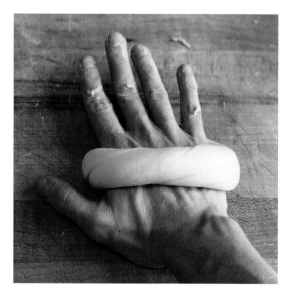

Day 2: Preheat the oven to 400°F. Remove the bagels from the refrigerator.

In a large, wide pot, combine the remaining 6 to 8 cups water and the remaining 1 tablespoon molasses. Bring the water to a rapid boil over high heat; lower the heat to a simmer. Place the bagels in the water, with the rounded top face down first. You can cook up to three bagels at a time if you have room in your pot. Simmer each bagel for 5 to 10 seconds on each side, then carefully use a slotted spoon or frying spider to transfer them, top up, to a baking sheet, about 2 to 3 inches apart: they will expand during baking. Sprinkle on topping, if using. (You can also place your topping in a wide bowl or plate, then flip the bagels straight from the pot into the topping, then place them on the baking sheet.)

Bake for about 15 minutes, or just until the bagels turn golden brown. Bagels will keep wrapped airtight at room temperature for up to 3 days.

FOR MY FAVORITE SPICY EVERYTHING MIX: Combine 1 tablespoon red pepper flakes, 1 tablespoon dried garlic, 1 tablespoon poppy seeds, 2 tablespoons dried onion, 2 tablespoons coarse sea salt, and 2 tablespoons sesame seeds. Store at room temperature.

BREAKFAST COOKIES

Makes 24 cookies

This is another easy one-bowl recipe. They keep forever in an airtight container and are a great guilt-free snack or an actual on-the-go breakfast treat. Who doesn't love almonds and oats?! I recommend that you use rolled oats, not the quick ones, which make a mushier cookie.

- 1 cup rolled oats or oat flour
- 1 cup sliced almonds (skin or no skin; you can also substitute almond flour)
- 1½ cups all-purpose or whole-grain flour (try rye or spelt to really mix it up)
- ½ teaspoon ground cinnamon
- ½ teaspoon kosher salt
- ½ cup maple syrup or agave
- ½ cup vegetable oil
- ½ cup jam, nut butter, or Nutella

Preheat the oven to 350°F. Line two baking sheets with parchment paper.

In a food processor or blender, add the oats and almonds and grind them into a flour. Transfer the mixture to a large mixing bowl. Stir in the flour, cinnamon, and salt. Add the maple syrup and oil and mix together until all the ingredients are incorporated.

Scoop tablespoons of dough and form into round balls. Place the balls 2 inches apart on the baking sheets. Use your knuckle to make a well in the center of each ball. Fill the well with 1 teaspoon jam or your preferred filling.

Bake for 8 minutes, until they are set just enough to pick up. If you overbake them, they will be rock-hard when they cool. Breakfast cookies will keep wrapped airtight at room temperature for up to 2 weeks.

MIX & MATCH MUFFINS

Makes 24 muffins

I like multipurpose recipes. Like pizza dough and brioche dough, this muffin batter has endless possibilities. It's a great way to use up bits and pieces of fruits, nuts, even veggies and herbs. They are moist, delicious, and great to grab for a breakfast treat. P.S.: The kids will eat them, especially if you add chocolate chips!

½ cup (1 stick) unsalted butter, at room temperature

1½ cups sugar

4 large eggs

1 cup Greek yogurt or sour cream

1 tablespoon vanilla extract

¼ cup vegetable oil

3 cups all-purpose flour

1½ teaspoons kosher salt

2 teaspoons baking powder

3 cups mix-ins of your choice (such as frozen fruit—don't defrost, fresh fruit, chocolate chips, or nuts), divided

Preheat the oven to 325°F. Grease 24 muffin cups with butter or use paper muffin liners.

In the bowl of a stand mixer fitted with a paddle attachment, cream the butter and sugar on medium-high speed, until light in color. Add the eggs one at a time; continue mixing on medium speed until each is incorporated.

Add the Greek yogurt, vanilla, and oil. Scrape the bottom of the bowl to make sure the ingredients are evenly distributed and mix the batter for 1 minute. Add the flour, salt, and baking powder. Mix on low speed until just barely combined.

Fold in 2½ cups of the mix-ins by hand. (Don't squish any berries!) Reserve ½ cup of the fun stuff to sprinkle on top of the muffins.

Spoon the batter into the muffin cups, filling each two-thirds full. Sprinkle the remaining mix-ins on top. Bake for about 30 minutes, or until a toothpick inserted in the center of a muffin comes out clean. Muffins will keep wrapped airtight at room temperature for up to 3 days.

Muffin Ideas

JUST BLUEBERRY: 3 cups blueberries

CHERRY ALMOND: 2 cups cherries, 1 cup sliced almonds

CHOCOLATE CHIP: 3 cups chocolate chips

TRIPLE BERRY: 1 cup blueberries, 1 cup raspberries, 1 cup blackberries

APPLE CRANBERRY: 2 cups diced apples, 1 cup fresh or dried cranberries

CORN MUFFINS: 3 cups fresh corn kernels, ¼ cup cornmeal, 1 tablespoon chives (or diced jalapenos)

PEANUT BUTTER COOKIES

These cookies happen to be flourless, making them an easy gluten-free option. They also happen to be quick and easy to throw together in one bowl when you need a sweet treat. I use natural, no-sugar-added peanut butter when I bake these, but the standard brands work, too. You can also swap the peanut butter with almond or sunflower seed butter; the cookies will spread more and have a slightly different texture after baking, but they will still be really yummy!

2 large eggs

1½ cups sugar

2 teaspoons baking soda

1 teaspoon vanilla extract

2 cups creamy peanut butter (preferably with no added sugar)

Chocolate chips (optional)

Preheat the oven to 325°F. Line a baking sheet with parchment paper.

In a large mixing bowl, whisk the eggs, sugar, baking soda, and vanilla together for about 60 seconds. When properly beaten, the mixture will be fluffy and light in color. (You can also use a stand mixer fitted with a whisk attachment, if you prefer.) Add the peanut butter and whisk until incorporated; the dough will become very stiff. If you choose to add chocolate chips, stir them in now.

Fill a bowl with additional sugar. Form tablespoon-sized balls of dough and roll them in the sugar; coat each ball completely. Place the balls 2 inches apart on the baking sheet. Use a fork to make a crisscross on the top of each ball. It's just for looks, but you can't have a peanut butter cookie without it, right? If you added chocolate chips, simply flatten the dough balls using the bottom of a glass.

Bake for 10 minutes. The cookies will still appear soft and underbaked, but rest assured they will set. Let them cool completely on the baking sheet. If you don't, they'll fall apart, you'll burn your fingers, and you'll wish you followed the directions. Cookies will keep wrapped airtight at room temperature for up to 10 days.

BANANA BREAD

Makes one 9 by 5-inch loaf, 10 mini loaves, or 12 to 18 muffins

This is my favorite banana bread recipe, and the best part is that you can make it using just one bowl! I think it's best with whole wheat flour, but if you don't have it, you can use all-purpose flour. If you think you don't like whole wheat flour, you might like this. My kids have NO idea I don't use white flour. Keegan asks me to make this for him almost daily. The bananas can be on the verge of edible and still work well for baking. If they're teetering on the brink and you're not ready to bake, throw them in the freezer—peels off!—and thaw before using them. The bananas Josie and I used today were straight from the freezer. They get a little watery, but that's okay.

⅔ cup vegetable oil

4 or 5 really ripe bananas (the more they ripen, the sweeter they get)

1¾ cups packed dark brown sugar, divided

2 large eggs

1 teaspoon vanilla extract

1½ cups whole wheat or all-purpose flour

1 teaspoon baking soda

½ teaspoon baking powder

¾ teaspoon kosher salt

2 teaspoons ground cinnamon, divided

1 cup mix-ins (such as chocolate chips, walnuts, raisins, or pecans; optional)

Preheat the oven to 350°F. Grease one 9 by 5-inch loaf pan, 10 mini loaf pans, or 12 to 18 muffins cups using vegetable oil (or use paper liners).

You only need ONE large mixing bowl! Add the oil, bananas, 1¼ cups of the brown sugar, eggs, and vanilla. Using a potato masher or your fingers, mash everything together. Add the flour, baking soda, baking powder, salt, and 1 teaspoon of the cinnamon and stir together. Add the mix-ins to the batter, if using.

Pour the batter into the prepared pan(s). To make the topping, combine the remaining ½ cup brown sugar and 1 teaspoon cinnamon in a small bowl. Sprinkle over the top.

Bake for about 45 minutes for one full-size loaf or 15 to 18 minutes for muffins and mini loaves, until a toothpick inserted in the middle comes out clean. Banana bread will keep wrapped airtight at room temperature for up to 5 days.

MEXICAN CHOCOLATE CAKE

This cake was how we celebrated Cinco de Mayo during the pandemic. We held a #MBCbakealong and invited our community to bake cakes together (separately). More than fifty people did! It was the perfect cake to make when we were all avoiding the grocery store, as it does not contain eggs or dairy (which makes it unintentionally vegan). It is based on a traditional "pantry" or "poor man's" cake, and it's definitely one you can give the kids to make—ONLY ONE BOWL required!! I started making this cake for potlucks in college, back when I was a vegan. Yes, it's true, I did my time, but I grew out of it years later when I started culinary school and I was determined to try everything! This cake is still one of my all-time favorite recipes. I like to top mine with strawberries, but you can use another type of fruit or keep it plain. If you prefer even more simple, you can leave out the spices.

Cake

1½ cups all-purpose flour

1 cup sugar

½ cup cocoa powder

1 teaspoon baking soda

¼ teaspoon kosher salt

2 teaspoons ground cinnamon

¼ teaspoon ground cayenne pepper (use chili powder if you don't have any)

1 cup cold water

¼ cup vegetable oil

1 tablespoon balsamic vinegar (any vinegar works!)

1 tablespoon vanilla extract

Chocolate Cake Glaze

Makes 1 cup glaze or enough to glaze one 8-inch round or 9-inch square cake

1 cup confectioners' sugar

½ cup cocoa powder

4 tablespoons water

Strawberries or other fresh fruit slices, for topping (optional)

Preheat the oven to 350°F. Grease a single 8-inch round or a 9-inch square pan with vegetable oil.

To make the cake, use a whisk or a wooden spoon to stir together the flour, sugar, cocoa powder, baking soda, salt, cinnamon, and cayenne pepper in a large bowl. Next, add the water, oil, balsamic vinegar, and vanilla, and stir until incorporated.

continued

continued from page 170

Pour the batter into the pan and bake for 25 to 30 minutes, until you can stick a knife in the center and pull it out clean.

To make the glaze, mix the confectioners' sugar, cocoa powder, and water together in a medium bowl until it's shiny and smooth. Once the cake is completely cool, pour the chocolate glaze over the cooled cake. Use a spoon or spatula to spread it around the top and let it drip down the edges.

Decorate the top of the cake with fruit, if desired. That's it—all done! You have a cake. It will keep wrapped airtight at room temperature for up to 3 days.

Acknowledgments

Along my journey, there have been a handful of brilliant women in the writing community who have helped me find the right words to tell my stories. Thank you Marissa Rothkopf Bates, Allison Task, Elisa Ung, and Jean Lucas and the team at Andrews McMeel! An extra special thanks to Allison and Joanne Chang who both introduced me to Stacey Glick, my incredible agent who believed in this project when no one else did. I am so grateful for this group of talented, smart ladies.

Amy Sherber and Sharon Burns Leader, thank you for nurturing me through the early years of my baking career. You paved the way for all the lady bakers to follow in your footsteps and you continue to light the path with the brightest rays of sunshine.

Jessica Woodward, my right and left hands, "thank you" isn't enough to acknowledge how grateful I am to have you as my business partner and my friend. I could not have done any of this without you by my side.

Thank you, Josie, Keegan, and Mac, for being my first taste-testers, strongest critics, and number-one fans. I am so proud to be your mom! And to Olive for getting thrown into the mix and rising to the challenge.

Thank you, Brad, for teaching me how to laugh again, helping me rediscover my creativity, and pushing me to be a better version of myself.

Thank you to my Dad, Jim Wyman, for taking my frenetic calls when I need someone to turn to who knows what it's like to run a small business. And to my mom, Barb, who continues to support both of us and all of our hair-brained ideas.

Thank you to my mother, Anna Ruth Tubman, for helping me to fill in all the gaps, find old photos, and reminisce over family recipes.

Thank you, Peter Lobel, for gifting me the pot that fried the first doughnut and for recognizing my full potential before I even knew it was there.

Thank you, Michael Richman, for all the loaves of bread, dipped in all the plates of oil while in deep discussions about things that probably didn't matter. I owe you, friend.

Thank you, Chef Nick Greco. Without you, I would have never made it out of Bakeshop 6.

Thank you for all the miles, Anne Arthur, and for calling me out on my shit and forever telling it like it is. I appreciate you and our 5 a.m. chats, through the best and the worst of it.

To my bakery team, you are the best of the best! Thank you for helping me with the recipes, the tests, the photoshoots, and the rest of the chaos to get the job done.

And finally, to the runners, YOU gathered, YOU joined in, YOU believed, YOU made this possible. YOU are my people. All my love and gratitude goes to YOU.

Metric Conversions and Equivalents

APPROXIMATE METRIC EQUIVALENTS

Volume

¼ teaspoon	1 milliliter
½ teaspoon	2.5 milliliters
¾ teaspoon	4 milliliters
1 teaspoon	5 milliliters
1¼ teaspoons	6 milliliters
1½ teaspoons	7.5 milliliters
1¾ teaspoons	8.5 milliliters
2 teaspoons	10 milliliters
1 tablespoon (½ fluid ounce)	15 milliliters
2 tablespoons (1 fluid ounce)	30 milliliters
¼ cup	60 milliliters
⅓ cup	80 milliliters
½ cup (4 fluid ounces)	120 milliliters
⅔ cup	160 milliliters
¾ cup	180 milliliters
1 cup (8 fluid ounces)	240 milliliters
1¼ cups	300 milliliters
1½ cups (12 fluid ounces)	360 milliliters
1⅔ cups	400 milliliters
2 cups (1 pint)	460 milliliters
3 cups	700 milliliters
4 cups (1 quart)	.95 liter
1 quart plus ¼ cup	1 liter
4 quarts (1 gallon)	3.8 liters

Weight

¼ ounce	7 grams
½ ounce	14 grams
¾ ounce	21 grams
1 ounce	28 grams
1¼ ounces	35 grams
1½ ounces	42.5 grams
1⅔ ounces	45 grams
2 ounces	57 grams
3 ounces	85 grams
4 ounces (¼ pound)	113 grams
5 ounces	142 grams
6 ounces	170 grams
7 ounces	198 grams
8 ounces (½ pound)	227 grams
16 ounces (1 pound)	454 grams
35.25 ounces (2.2 pounds)	1 kilogram

Length

⅛ inch	3 millimeters
¼ inch	6 millimeters
½ inch	1¼ centimeters
1 inch	2½ centimeters
2 inches	5 centimeters
2½ inches	6 centimeters
4 inches	10 centimeters
5 inches	13 centimeters
6 inches	15¼ centimeters
12 inches (1 foot)	30 centimeters

METRIC CONVERSION FORMULAS

To Convert	Multiply
Ounces to grams	Ounces by 28.35
Pounds to kilograms	Pounds by .454
Teaspoons to milliliters	Teaspoons by 4.93
Tablespoons to milliliters	Tablespoons by 14.79
Fluid ounces to milliliters	Fluid ounces by 29.57
Cups to milliliters	Cups by 236.59
Cups to liters	Cups by .236
Pints to liters	Pints by .473
Quarts to liters	Quarts by .946
Gallons to liters	Gallons by 3.785
Inches to centimeters	Inches by 2.54

OVEN TEMPERATURES

To convert Fahrenheit to Celsius, subtract 32 from Fahrenheit, multiply the result by 5, then divide by 9.

Description	Fahrenheit	Celsius	British Gas Mark
Very cool	200°	95°	0
Very cool	225°	110°	¼
Very cool	250°	120°	½
Cool	275°	135°	1
Cool	300°	150°	2
Warm	325°	165°	3
Moderate	350°	175°	4
Moderately hot	375°	190°	5
Fairly hot	400°	200°	6
Hot	425°	220°	7
Very hot	450°	230°	8
Very hot	475°	245°	9

COMMON INGREDIENTS AND THEIR APPROXIMATE EQUIVALENTS

1 cup uncooked white rice = 185 grams

1 cup all-purpose flour = 125 grams

1 stick butter (4 ounces • ½ cup • 8 tablespoons) = 115 grams

1 cup butter (8 ounces • 2 sticks • 16 tablespoons) = 225 grams

1 cup brown sugar, firmly packed = 220 grams

1 cup granulated sugar = 200 grams

Information compiled from a variety of sources, including *Recipes into Type* by Joan Whitman and Dolores Simon (Newton, MA: Biscuit Books, 1993); *The New Food Lover's Companion* by Sharon Tyler Herbst (Hauppauge, NY: Barron's, 2013); and *Rosemary Brown's Big Kitchen Instruction Book* (Kansas City, MO: Andrews McMeel, 1998).

Index

About the Author

Rachel Wyman grew up in Maryland and as a child watched her grandmother make wedding cakes. After graduating from the University of Florida with a French degree, she studied baking and pastry at the Culinary Institute of America in Hyde Park, NY, where she discovered a passion for baking bread. She felt "there was a soulfulness about it that wasn't found in fancy cakes." She has worked for Bread Alone Bakery, Amy's Bread, and the Ritz-Carlton and has developed bread recipes for Wegmans, Whole Foods, Target, and Starbucks.

Nine months after she opened Montclair Bread Company in New Jersey in 2012, business was stale. She had spent years rising before dawn to perfect the combination of flour, water, yeast, and salt, and she had the bread to prove it. But on a good day, only thirty people trickled through her door, until one Sunday morning when one of her bakers asked her to make doughnuts. This was risky because her customers often begged for healthy foods. The doughnuts sold out in minutes, and the number of customers continued to grow along with the line for doughnuts that stretched to the end of the block.

In 2014, she won The Cooking Channel's "Donut Showdown" competition. In 2015, *Bake Magazine* named her "One of the 25 Most Influential Bakers in the US." In 2016, she was featured in the *New York Times* story "Montclair Bread Company has Sunday Treats All Week Long."

Her business flourished until the global pandemic in 2020. Rachel had no choice but to adapt to keep her business going and even started a virtual bake-a-long to help support and communicate with the community during the lockdowns. She also recently wrote about the struggles of operating a business during the pandemic for CNN Business Perspectives.

This book shares the tried-and-true recipes Rachel spent three decades perfecting that are now the backbone of her bakery. Recipes include her childhood favorite, Mombo's Carrot Cake; a large variety of her famous brioche doughnuts; community favorites such as her pizza and energy bars; and, finally, quarantine staples such as tortillas and cheese crackers. Rachel brings joy to baking, makes yeast less scary, and helps home bakers make the perfect dough under any conditions. This is a story of how her love of baking brought a community together and held it together during a global pandemic. Montclair Bread Company not only offers bountiful baked treats to throngs of fans and is a mecca for runners who line up each year to race for doughnuts, it is the embodiment of resilience and adapting to survive a crisis. Rachel resides in Montclair, NJ, with her three children and a giant long-eared rabbit named Prim.

Will Run for Doughnuts

Andrews McMeel Publishing
a division of Andrews McMeel Universal
1130 Walnut Street, Kansas City, Missouri 64106

www.andrewsmcmeel.com
www.montclairbread.com

21 22 23 24 25 SHO 10 9 8 7 6 5 4 3 2 1

ISBN: 978-1-5248-6764-5

Library of Congress Control Number: 2021936972

Editor: Jean Lucas
Art Director/Designer: Holly Swayne
Photographer: Brad Barket
Production Editor: Margaret Daniels
Production Manager: Carol Coe

Attention: Schools and Businesses
Andrews McMeel books are available at quantity discounts with bulk purchase
for educational, business, or sales promotional use. For information, please e-mail the
Andrews McMeel Publishing Special Sales Department:
specialsales@amuniversal.com.